TENNYSON
& HIS POETRY

Alfred, Lord Tennyson

TENNYSON
& HIS POETRY

BY

R. BRIMLEY JOHNSON

KENNIKAT PRESS
Port Washington, N. Y./London

TENNYSON & HIS POETRY

First published in 1913
Reissued in 1970 by Kennikat Press
Library of Congress Catalog Card No: 71-103196
SBN 8046-0833-4

Manufactured by Taylor Publishing Company   Dallas, Texas

GENERAL PREFACE

A GLANCE through the pages of this little book will suffice to disclose the general plan of the series of which it forms a part. Only a few words of explanation, therefore, will be necessary.

The point of departure is the undeniable fact that with the vast majority of young students of literature a living interest in the work of any poet can best be aroused, and an intelligent appreciation of it secured, when it is immediately associated with the character and career of the poet himself. The cases are indeed few and far between in which much fresh light will not be thrown upon a poem by some knowledge of the personality of the writer, while it will often be found that the most direct—perhaps even the only—way to the heart of its meaning lies through a consideration of the circumstances in which it had its birth. The purely æsthetic critic may possibly object that a poem should be regarded simply as a self-contained and detached piece of art, having no personal affiliations or bearings. Of the validity of this as an abstract principle nothing need now be said. The fact remains that, in the earlier stages of study at any rate, poetry is most valued and loved when it is made to seem most human and vital ; and the human and vital interest of poetry can be most surely brought home to the reader by the biographical method of interpretation.

GENERAL PREFACE

This is to some extent recognised by writers of histories and text-books of literature, and by editors of selections from the works of our poets ; for place is always given by them to a certain amount of biographical material. But in the histories and text-books the biography of a given writer stands by itself, and his work has to be sought elsewhere, the student being left to make the connexion for himself ; while even in our current editions of selections there is little systematic attempt to link biography, step by step, with production.

This brings us at once to the chief purpose of the present series. In this, biography and production will be considered together and in intimate association. In other words, an endeavour will be made to interest the reader in the lives and personalities of the poets dealt with, and at the same time to use biography as an introduction and key to their writings.

Each volume will therefore contain the life-story of the poet who forms its subject. In this, attention will be specially directed to his personality as it expressed itself in his poetry, and to the influences and conditions which counted most as formative factors in the growth of his genius. This biographical study will be used as a setting for a selection, as large as space will permit, of his representative poems. Such poems, where possible, will be reproduced in full, and care will be taken to bring out their connexion with his character, his circumstances, and the movement of his mind. Then, in

GENERAL PREFACE

addition, so much more general literary criticism will be incorporated as may seem to be needed to supplement the biographical material, and to exhibit both the essential qualities and the historical importance of his work.

It is believed that the plan thus pursued is substantially in the nature of a new departure, and that the volumes of this series, constituting as they will an introduction to the study of some of our greatest poets, will be found useful to teachers and students of literature, and no less to the general lover of English poetry.

WILLIAM HENRY HUDSON

POEMS QUOTED
IN WHOLE

POEMS QUOTED
IN PART

POEMS QUOTED

TENNYSON
& HIS POETRY

ONE of the few Poets Laureate who were
also poets, Tennyson is perhaps the most
typical genius of the Victorian era in its
maturity. There is a sense in which he was
pre-eminent among those greater than himself.
He presents the art of his age, as Queen
Victoria exemplified its domestic, and Gladstone
its political, morality. He stands for that stage
in the development of civilization which believed,
with enthusiasm, in its own discoveries and
panaceas ; that liberalism which fought for
progress without contemplating a change in
the direction of advance ; that faith which
glorified the love of man.

Yet Tennyson was before all a poet, a seer
of visions. The gift of recognizing beauty and
goodness behind the clouds of the present gave
him a hold on popular imagination which
did more, perhaps, for humanity than those
dreams of a Utopian future, or regrets for the
past, which are the usual preoccupations of the
artist. Just because, if in front, he was not
in advance of his age, because he upheld what
was noblest and best in the art, morality, and
intellect of his day, Tennyson was able to
purify common thought, to stir ordinary men.
Extolling the power of machinery, boasting of
scientific research, and hopeful concerning the

responsibilities of wealth, he was never materialistic and held no brief for commercial tyranny.

Tennyson was before all things a flawless artist ; he spared no pains toward the perfection of style ; he had faith in the poet's mission. It is well that genius should recognize its own importance and refuse the distractions of convention. It should concern itself exclusively, as he did, with the exaltation of the Ideal.

Tennyson's work is permeated with idealism, the idealism of the English gentleman, the Victorian knight-errant, most finally and fully expressed by " In Memoriam " and the " Idylls." We shall find, in studying this work, a fine unity of purpose, an underlying motive, that reveals the man. Thus he lives as a complete, consistent force : with a meaning and value for all time. He sings the message of Victorianism.

II

ALFRED, Lord Tennyson, of Aldworth, Sussex, and of Freshwater, Isle of Wight, was born in his father's rectory of Somersby, Lincolnshire, on August 6, 1809. The family claim Danish descent, having first settled in Holderness, north of the Humber. In 1343 we find a John Tenison complaining of robbery ; in 1528 a John Tennyson leaves directions about his burial and his possessions. Thence, through one Launcelot Tennyson of

Preston, and Ralph, supporter of William III,
we reach the great-grandfather of the poet.

Tennyson's own father, the Rev. Dr. George
Clayton Tennyson, was disinherited, apparently
from mere caprice, and had no real calling for
the Church. Obviously the injustice weighed
on him through life, producing a stern despon-
dency which partially detracted from the influence of his dominating intellect. Alfred,
the fourth of twelve children, had certainly a
sound classical training and the free run of an
excellent library.

His mother has been described as " a remarkable and saintly woman."

> The world hath not another
> (Tho' all her fairest forms are types of thee,
> And thou of God in thy great charity)
> Of such a finish'd, chasten'd purity.

She had been a beauty, delighted her children by
her sense of humour, and inspired them with
that love of animals, that pity " for all wounded
wings " which distinguished her son's work.

Other members of the household presented
singular contrasts that made things exciting for
young people. A Calvinist aunt, Mrs. Bourne,
wept to think that God had " damned most
of her friends " ; while the cook said of her
master and mistress that " If you raked out
hell with a small-tooth comb you won't find
their likes."

Moreover, the boy was always sensitive to the
influences of nature. The fenlands of Lincoln-

shire, their moors, watercourses and pools, are
reflected in many a line of his early verse. It
was the rectory lawn, on which he wrote "A
spirit haunts the year's last hours," beyond
which stood

> A garden bower'd close
> With plaited alleys of the trailing rose,
> Long alleys falling down to twilight grots,
> Or opening upon level plots
> Of crowned lilies, standing near
> Purple-spiked lavender;

while further on flowed the Sowersby stream
(*not* the original of "The Brook") which
inspired "Flow down, cold rivulet, to the sea."

The young Alfred was a great teller of stories,
legendary or adventurous, and his family
thought he would turn out an actor. From
seven to eleven he lived with his grandmother at
Louth, and went to the Grammar School, where
flogging was perpetual, but afterwards studied
with his father till entering Cambridge.

Tennyson's grandfather once asked the boy
to write a poem on his grandmother's death, and
paid him for it, with the oft-quoted comment:
"Here is half a guinea for you, the first you
have ever earned by poetry and, take my word
for it, the last." But he was not, in fact, a
precocious writer. His earliest published
volumes are not above, if they equal, the average
poetry which many of us write in youth; they
contain some strikingly poor verses which, it
is hardly necessary to add, were never re-

printed by their author ; nor, *pace* the late
Master of Balliol, can we find greater merit in
the fragmentary Poems of Boyhood which first
appeared in his son's " Life."

III

THOUGH one would not, perhaps, call
Tennyson an academic poet, there is no
doubt that his life at Cambridge had considerable permanent influence on his character
and his work.　He made several friends there of
exceptional mental calibre, and always retained
an affectionate enthusiasm for his experience
as an undergraduate.

Alfred and Charles Tennyson entered Trinity
on February 20, 1828, their elder brother,
Frederick, being already a distinguished scholar
of the same college.　Though naturally shy and
reserved, they soon made their way into a con-
genial set, who were all keen literary critics and
eager politicians. Perhaps they were most
influenced, at the time, by Coleridge, Wordsworth, and Carlyle.

Tennyson himself was the hero of the group,
" six feet high, broad-chested, strong-limbed, his
face Shakespearian, with deep eyelids, his ample
forehead, crowned with dark wavy hair, his head
finely poised, his hand the admiration of sculp-
tors, long fingers with square tips, soft as a
child's, but of great size and strength." Thomp-
son, afterwards Master, said of him at first sight,
" that man must be a poet."

15

TENNYSON & HIS POETRY

The record that he " saw the moonlight reflected in a nightingale's eye, as she was singing in the hedgerow " (inspiring the " leaves that tremble round the nightingale " in the " Gardener's Daughter "), belongs to this period. The sonnet which Hallam declared " worth an estate in Golconda " celebrates the same experience :

> Check every outflash, every ruder sally
> Of thought and speech, speak low, and give up
>   wholly
> Thy spirit to mild-minded Melancholy :
> This is the place.   Thro' yonder poplar alley,
> Below, the green river windeth slowly ;
> But in the middle of the sombre valley,
> The crispèd waters whisper musically,
> And all the haunted place is dark and holy.
> The nightingale, with long and low preamble,
> Warbled from yonder knoll of solemn larches,
> And in and out the woodbine's flowery arches
> The summer midges wove their wanton gambol,
> And all the white-stemm'd pinewood slept above,
> When in this valley first I told my love.

But the young Alfred never devoted himself exclusively to gazing in nightingale's eyes or other poetic dreaming. He was a vigorous walker, very muscular, and fond of athletics in many forms. The enthusiasms of Cambridge, moreover, carried him toward any honourable fight for liberty ; so that, in 1830, we find him and Hallam embarked for the Pyrenees with money to support Torrigos in his revolt against

16

Ferdinand and the Inquisition. The friends
joined secret meetings and were reported
" missing " for a few weeks. Passing through
France, Tennyson emphasized the light-hearted-
ness of our Gallic neighbours ; and preferred
always the " freer air of England." " Some
one says," he wrote, " that nothing strikes a
traveller more on returning from the Continent
than the look of an English country town.
Houses not so big, nor such rows of them as
abroad, but each man's house, little or big dis-
tance from one another, his own castle, built
according to his own means and fancy, and so
indicating the Englishman's free individual
humour. I am struck on returning from France
with the look of good sense in the London
people." Yet we learn that on the Continent he
was never taken for an Englishman ; and in
Ireland he was assumed to be French—planning
" a revolution " !

From undergraduate days Tennyson seems to
have impressed his personality on all who came
into anything like intimate association with
him ; and, in 1822 (the date of his second
volume), we find references to " the great
Alfred," while the same year found a " question
put up at the Cambridge Union, ' Tennyson or
Milton, which the greater poet ? ' "

The now historic " Poems by Two Brothers,"
1827 (actually written by Alfred, Charles, and
the elder, Frederick), need not detain us. The
Laureate himself refers to it as " early rot," and
the work is almost entirely imitative. But the

short interval between these and "Poems chiefly
Lyrical," 1830, reveals extraordinary advance,
for these are, as Aubrey de Vere declared,
"eminently original," with "a wild, inexplicable
magic and a deep pathos." The young poet
favoured the elaborate and somewhat artificial
diction of his time ; and showed little concern
with life's realities. Still, he had learnt already
to control the luxuriance of his imagination ; he
had observed what he describes, and he struck a
true lyrical note. We read the first "Mariana"
and the "Arabian Nights" with pleasure,
though nothing here approaches "The Miller's
Daughter," "The Palace of Art," or "The
Dream of Fair Women" of only two years
later.

It is, indeed, with the appearance of "Poems"
by Alfred Tennyson, 1832, that his career may
be said to have seriously begun, the final bent
of his genius to have been actually determined.
One may say frankly that he did not actually
start with any particular distinction, but, on the
other hand, he matured early. It was probably
the poet's instinct for self-measurement which
restrained his ambition ; for we still find no
elaborately sustained effort or really long poem.
He continues the lyric form (possibly a trifle less
"faultless") in higher flight, and the homely
narrative : the new features being, in the main,
philosophical.

As Spedding put it, " Not only was the aim
generally larger, the subjects and interest more
substantial, and the endeavour more sustained,

18

but the original and distinctive character of the man appeared more plainly. His genius was manifestly shaping a peculiar course for itself, and finding out its proper business ; the moral soul was beginning more and more to assume its due predominance, not in the way of formal preaching (the proper vehicle of which is prose), but in the shape and colour which his creations unconsciously took, and the feelings which they were made insensibly to suggest.''

This was most marked in the poem in which Tennyson himself, probably, bestowed most care : the protest against Pride, entitled '' The Palace of Art,'' with its marvellously compressed word-pictures. He calls it the '' embodiment of my own belief that the godlike life is with man and for man.'' It exposes the heresy, then novel, of Art for Art's sake ; subordinating man's work to Nature and Religion.

> Beauty, Good and Knowledge are three sisters . . .
> And never can be sunder'd without tears.
> And he that shuts out Love, in turn shall be
> Shut out from Love, and on her threshold lie,
> Howling in outer darkness.

The '' god-like isolation '' of the Palace, which is *not* a temple ('' created by the imagination exclusively for its own delight, an imagination so great that it refuses all human sympathy ''), reveals extraordinary '' vividness and concentrated power.'' The descriptions of sculpture, intended to be more numerous than they actually were, are peculiarly characteristic.

After four years the soul "threw her royal robes away" :

> "Make me a cottage in the vale," she said,
> "Where I may mourn and pray."

Poems more characteristic of work one generally associates with the Laureate, and destined perhaps to sounder fame, belong to this volume. "The May Queen" is more widely known than its own author, the visionary "Dream of Fair Women" is supreme of its kind, the luxurious "Lotus-Eaters" never sacrifices unity to beauty.

And Tennyson lives most in the magic symbolism of "The Lady of Shalott," "Mariana" of Southern France, and such world-famed idylls as "The Miller's Daughter," which are distinguished, beyond their obviously popular appeal, by the exact harmony between landscape and humanity.

Here, moreover, were included "two short poems of extraordinary strength and majesty," beginning "You ask me, why, tho' ill at ease," and "Of old sat Freedom on the heights." Their massive perfection of form—suggesting a sculptor's art more than a painter's—is no less characteristic than their political teaching, wherein liberty, however passionately beloved, is yet set on high as a moral power of wisdom and self-control, distrusting a tyrant majority.

> It is the land that freemen till,
>   That sober-suited Freedom chose,
>   The land, where girt with friends or foes
> A man may speak the thing he will ;

A land of settled government,
   A land of just and old renown,
   Where Freedom slowly broadens down
From precedent to precedent :

Where faction seldom gathers head,
   But by degrees to fullness wrought,
   The strength of some diffusive thought
Hath time and space to work and spread.

It was his candid friend Spedding who, having
said that " Alfred continued writing, like a
crocodile, sideways and onward," declared the
real fault in his early work to be " the tendency,
arising from the fullness of a mind which had
not yet learned to master its resources freely,
to overcrowd his composition with imagery, to
which may be added an over-indulgence in the
luxuries of the senses, a profusion of splendours,
harmonies, perfumes, gorgeous apparel, luscious
meats and drinks, and ' creature comforts '
which rather pall upon the sense, and make the
glories of the outward world a little to obscure
and overshadow the world within."

IV

IF the 1832 volume brought Tennyson before
the thoughtful few, it was not until ten
years later that he can fairly be said to
have caught the public ear. The interval witnessed perhaps the most significant event in
his private life—Arthur Hallam's death. The

promise of Hallam *may* have been exaggerated by his intimate friends, but the man who inspired " In Memoriam " won other admirers, and will live for ever in the memory of all. He was engaged to Tennyson's sister, and the friendship stands out in literary annals as an everlasting monument of faithful devotion without sentimentality.

Through the marriage of Charles Tennyson to Louisa Sellwood the poet became intimate with her sister Emily, the future Lady Tennyson, though they were not married till 1850, when she brought " the peace of God into his life before the altar." Then too began apparently that intimate study and reflection upon the other Arthur, the perfect gentleman of England. " How much of history," he writes, " we have in the story of Arthur is doubtful. Let not my readers press too hardly on details, whether for history or allegory. Some think that King Arthur may be taken to typify conscience. He is anyhow meant to be a man who spent himself in the cause of honour, duty and self-sacrifice, who felt and aspired with his nobler knights, though with a stronger and a clearer conscience than any of them, ' reverencing his conscience as his king.' ' There was no such perfect man since Adam,' as an old writer says. ' Major præteritis majorque futuris regibus.' "

Tennyson had already entered upon that extreme devotion to the cultivation of language which made his work so flawless, each volume always appearing more perfect technically than its predecessor, and his life being apparently so colourless because so single-minded. He was already at work on the revision of such earlier poems as he considered worthy of preservation, a habit which stayed with him till death. If, as may well be, the loss of his friend deadened any ambition for an active or public life, it never diminished his power for thought or his passion for humanity ; he never allowed it to grow into an excuse for idleness. The next volumes might otherwise have appeared earlier ; they could scarcely have been less characteristic, less worthy, or less full of hope.

Thus after the silence of sorrow came song, and the 1842 volumes awakened the world to its possession of a new poet, with their noble group of " English Idylls," with " St. Simeon Stylites," the eager " Locksley Hall," and a few fragments of the Arthur cycle—the " Morte d'Arthur," " Sir Galahad," "Sir Launcelot and Queen Guinevere."

The revision of early work revealed great judgment, being " always with a view to strip off redundancies, to make the expression simpler and clearer, to substitute thought for imagery, and substance for shadow." As Aubrey de Vere put it :

" It was the heart of England even more than her imagination that he made his own. It was the Humanities and the truths underlying them that he sang, and he so sang them that any deep-hearted reader was made to feel through his far-reaching thought that those Humanities are

23

TENNYSON & HIS POETRY

spiritual things, and that to touch them is to touch the garment of the Divine. Those who confer so deep a benefit cannot but be remembered. The Heroic is not greatly appreciated in these days ; but on this occasion the challenge met with response."

Now " his name was on every one's lips, his poems discussed, criticized, interpreted ; portions of them repeatedly set for translation into Latin or Greek verse at schools and colleges ; read and re-read so repeatedly that there were many of us who could repeat page after page from memory." Carlyle found in them " the pulse of a real man's heart " :—" a right valiant, true fighting, victorious heart ; strong as a lion's, yet gentle, loving and full of music : what I call a genuine singer's heart ! There are tunes as of the nightingale ; low murmurs as of wood-doves at summer noon ; everywhere a noble sound as of the free winds and leafy woods. The sunniest glow of life dwells in that soul, chequered duly with dark streaks from night and Hades : everywhere one feels as if all were filled with yellow glowing sunlight, some glorious golden vapour ; from which form after form bodies itself ; naturally, *golden* forms. In one word there seems to be a note of ' The Eternal Melodies ' in this man : for which let all other men be thankful and joyful."

" Dora " reminds him of the book of Ruth, the " Two Voices " brings to mind passages of Job, the " Talking Oak " is " kindred to something that is best in Goethe." " Besides," as

24

TENNYSON & HIS POETRY

Mrs. Carlyle has it, " he is a very handsome man " : " a great shock of rough dusky dark hair, bright laughing hazel eyes ; massive aquiline face, most massive, yet most delicate ; of sallow brown complexion, almost Indian-looking ; clothes cynically loose, free-and-easy, smokes infinite tobacco. His voice is musical, metallic, fit for loud laughter and piercing wail, and all that may lie between ; speech and speculation free and plenteous."

Most characteristic here, perhaps, of his own age (he was now thirty-three), and of the period, is " Locksley Hall " with its fine scorn of the " shallow-hearted," its ringing appeal to youth's dreaming :

When I dipt into the future far as human eye could
    see ;
Saw the Vision of the world, and all the wonder that
    would be.——

    *   *   *   *   *

Men, my brothers, men the workers, ever reaping
    something new :
That which they have done but earnest of the things
    that they shall do :

For I dipt into the future, far as human eye could see,
Saw the Vision of the world and all the wonder that
    would be ;

Saw the heavens fill with commerce, argosies of magic
    sails,
Pilots of the purple twilight, dropping down with costly
    bales

TENNYSON & HIS POETRY

Heard the heavens fill with shouting, and there rain'd
  a ghastly dew
From the nations' airy navies grappling in the central
  blue ;

Far along the world-wide whisper of the south-wind
  rushing warm,
With the standards of the peoples plunging thro' the
  thunder-storm ;

Till the war-drum throbb'd no longer, and the battle
  flags were furl'd
In the Parliament of man, the Federation of the
  world.

There the common sense of most shall hold a fretful
  realm in awe,
And the kindly earth shall slumber, lapt in universal
  law.

Or in another mood :

                              Ah, for some retreat
Deep in yonder shining Orient, where my life began to
  beat ;

Where in wild Mahratta-battle fell my father evil-
  starr'd ; —
I was left a trampled orphan, and a selfish uncle's
  ward.

Or to burst all links of habit—there to wander far
  away,
On from island unto island at the gateways of the
  day.

26

Larger constellations burning, mellow moons and
    happy skies,
Breadths of tropic shade and palms in cluster, knots
    of Paradise.

Never comes the trader, never floats an European
    flag,
Slides the bird o'er lustrous woodland, swings the
    trailer from the crag ;

Droops the heavy-blossom'd bower, hangs the heavy-
    fruited tree—
Summer isles of Eden lying in dark-purple spheres
    of sea.

There methinks would be enjoyment more than in
    this march of mind,
In the steamship, in the railway, in the thoughts that
    shake mankind.

There the passions cramp'd no longer shall have
    scope and breathing-space ;
I will take some savage woman, she shall rear my
    dusky race.

Iron-jointed, supple-sinew'd, they shall dive, and they
    shall run,
Catch the wild goat by the hair, and hurl their lances
    in the sun ;

Whistle back the parrot's call, and leap the rainbows
    of the brooks,
Not with blinded eyesight poring over miserable
    books—

Verily youth was not dead in the man who,
after the cynicism bred of love rejected, could

TENNYSON & HIS POETRY

thus paint the visions of a young dreamer ; and if the mood were passing, it yet speaks. For Tennyson has taught us that man should never sleep, never despair ; while hating also the false and the conventional, should fight on always for some ideal nobler than that lost to him through the cold calculations of others.

His ideal, indeed, was awake already in King Arthur,

> Like a modern gentleman of stateliest port,

and in Galahad's " virgin heart " :

> A maiden knight—to me is given
>   Such hope, I know not fear ;
> I yearn to breathe the airs of heaven
>   That often meet me here.
> I muse on joy that will not cease,
>   Pure spaces clothed in living beams,
> Pure lilies of eternal peace,
>   Whose odours haunt my dreams ;
> And, stricken by an angel's hand,
>   This mortal armour that I wear,
> This weight and size, this heart and eyes,
>   Are touch'd, are turn'd to finest air.

" Ulysses," again (a converse of the lesson taught in " The Lotus-Eaters "), shows what Heroism, prompted by no more than the " love of knowledge and the scorn of sloth," may be even in old age :

ULYSSES

> It little profits that an idle king,
> By this still hearth, among these barren crags,
> Match'd with an aged wife, I mete and dole

Unequal laws unto a savage race,
That hoard, and sleep, and feed, and know not me.
I cannot rest from travel : I will drink
Life to the lees : all times I have enjoy'd
Greatly, have suffer'd greatly, both with those
That loved me, and alone ; on shore, and when
Thro' scudding drifts the rainy Hyades
Vext the dim sea : I am become a name ;
For always roaming with a hungry heart
Much have I seen and known ; cities of men
And manners, climates, councils, governments,
Myself not least, but honour'd of them all ;
And drunk delight of battle with my peers,
Far on the ringing plains of windy Troy.
I am a part of all that I have met ;
Yet all experience is an arch wherethro'
Gleams that untravell'd world, whose margin fades
For ever and for ever when I move.
How dull it is to pause, to make an end,
To rust unburnish'd, not to shine in use !
As tho' to breathe were life.   Life piled on life
Were all too little, and of one to me
Little remains : but every hour is saved
From that eternal silence, something more
A bringer of new things ; and vile it were
For some three suns to store and hoard myself,
And this gray spirit yearning in desire
To follow knowledge like a sinking star,
Beyond the utmost bound of human thought.
   This is my son, mine own Telemachus,
To whom I leave the sceptre and the isle—
Well-loved of me, discerning to fulfil
This labour, by slow prudence to make mild
A rugged people, and thro' soft degrees
Subdue them to the useful and the good.

Most blameless is he, centred in the sphere
Of common duties, decent not to fail
In offices of tenderness, and pay
Meet adoration to my household gods,
When I am gone.   He works his work, I mine.
  There lies the port : the vessel puffs her sail :
There gloom the dark broad seas.   My mariners,
Souls that have toil'd, and wrought, and thought
      with me—
That ever with a frolic welcome took
The thunder and the sunshine, and opposed
Free hearts, free foreheads—you and I are old ;
Old age hath yet his honour and his toil ;
Death closes all : but something ere the end,
Some work of noble note, may yet be done,
Not unbecoming men that strove with Gods.
The lights begin to twinkle from the rocks :
The long day wanes : the slow moon climbs : the
      deep
Moans round with many voices.   Come, my friends,
'Tis not too late to seek a newer world.
Push off, and sitting well in order smite
The sounding furrows ; for my purpose holds
To sail beyond the sunset, and the baths
Of all the western stars, until I die.
It may be that the gulfs will wash us down :
It may be we shall touch the Happy Isles,
And see the great Achilles, whom we knew.
Tho' much is taken, much abides ; and tho'
We are not now that strength which in old days
Moved earth and heaven ; that which we are, we
      are ;
One equal temper of heroic hearts,
Made weak by time and fate, but strong in will
To strive, to seek, to find, and not to yield.

TENNYSON & HIS POETRY

TENNYSON & HIS POETRY

Tennyson himself considered that this poem (written soon after Hallam's death) " gave his feeling about the need of going forward, and braving the struggle of life perhaps more simply than anything in ' In Memoriam.' "

In Tennyson's mind Heaven was ever hovering round us, by the English wayside ; God shone through the eyes of man : chivalry lingered in modern everyday existence, with " Dora " and " The Gardener's Daughter."

> The rain had fallen, the Poet arose,
>   He pass'd by the town and out of the street,
> A light wind blew from the gates of the sun,
>   And waves of shadow went over the wheat,
> And he sat him down in a lonely place
>   And chanted a melody loud and sweet,
> That made the wild-swan pause in her cloud,
>   And the lark drop down at his feet.

If at times either restless or dreamy, after the manner of his age, Tennyson understood very well what " constitutes a sound condition of the soul." As in " The Palace of Art " he had already painted " the pride of voluptuous enjoyment," and in " The Two Voices " had exposed the cowardice of contemplated suicide, he now drew for us the " pride of ascetism at its basest " in the " coughs, aches and stitches " of St. Simeon Stylites ; so dramatically contrasted with " the end here and hereafter of the merely sensual man " in " The Vision of Sin."

Truly, Simeon,

> The watcher on the column till the end

had much trust in these " lower voices " of
silly people which shouted, " Behold a saint ! "

> Can I work miracles and not be saved ?

Yet was he more fool and less Christian than
they, with his chain'd leg, rope, goatskin, and
iron collar :

> To make me an example to mankind
> Which few can reach to.

The very riot of Penitence had blinded his eyes
to the true " vision of sin " and " the company
with heated eyes . . . at a ruin'd inn," swing-
ing themselves to " low voluptuous music."

> Thou shalt not be saved by works :
>   Thou hast been a sinner too :
> Ruin'd trunks on wither'd forks,
>   Empty scarecrows, I and you !
>
> We are men of ruin'd blood ;
>   Therefore comes it we are wise.
> Fish are we that love the mud,
>   Rising to no fancy-flies.
>
> Trooping from their mouldy dens
>   The chap-fallen circle spreads :
> Welcome, fellow-citizens,
>   Hollow hearts and empty heads !
>
> You are bones, and what of that
>   Every face, however full,
> Padded round with flesh and fat,
>   Is but modell'd on a skull.

Fill the cup, and fill the can !
  Mingle madness, mingle scorn !
Dregs of life, and lees of man :
  Yet we will not die forlorn.

To which an answer peal'd from that high land,
But in a tongue no man could understand ;
And on the glimmering limit far withdrawn
God made Himself an awful rose of dawn.

Having uttered his scorn of madness, Tennyson
turns, willingly enough, unto

                The Master, Love,
      A more ideal Artist he than all,

at whose touch " the common mouth, so gross
to express delight, grew oratory."

      Not wholly in the busy world, nor quite
      Beyond it, blooms the garden that I love.
      News from the humming city comes to it
      In sound of funeral or of marriage bells ;
      And, sitting muffled in dark leaves, you hear
      The windy clanging of the minster clock :
      Although between it and the garden lies
      A league of grass, wash'd by a slow broad
          stream,
      That, stirr'd with languid pulses of the oar,
      Waves all its lazy lilies, and creeps on,
      Barge-laden, to three arches of a bridge
      Crown'd with the minster-towers.

" In that still place," " grew, seldom seen,"
the fair "Gardener's Daughter," " a sight
to make an old man young." There youth

c

woo'd and, after "meetings and farewells," won "perfect Joy."

> Then, in that time and place, I spoke to her,
> Requiring, tho' I knew it was mine own,
> Yet for the pleasure that I took to hear,
> Requiring at her hand the greatest gift,
> A woman's heart, the heart of her I loved ;
> And in that time and place she answer'd me,
> And in the compass of three little words,
> More musical than ever came in one,
> The silver fragments of a broken voice,
> Made me most happy, faltering " I am thine."

On " Dora," " Audley Court," " The Talking Oak," " Lady Clare," " The Lord of Burleigh," or " Edward Gray," it is not necessary to dwell at length. All reflect similar " characteristic features of English life : so true to nature and to fact, with so careful a regard to perspective and to light and shade, that the simplicity of the result sometimes hides the art that has been exercised." They all reveal the master's and the lover's hand, in miniature scene-painting ; always subordinate, however, to human interest. We have already noted examples of his sympathy in the observation of detail. Another may here be noted.

" Audley Court," he has written, was " partially suggested by Abbey Park in Torquay," where " in those old days, coming down from the hill, he saw a star of phosphorescence made by the buoy appearing and disappearing in the dark sea." Yet the South Coast did not offer

him a " grand sea," only " an angry, curt sea,"
which " seems to shriek as it recoils with the
pebbles along the shore."—" The finest seas
I have ever seen are at Valencia, Mablethorpe and
in West Cornwall. At Valencia the sea was
grand, without any wind blowing and seemingly
without a wave, but with the momentum of the
Atlantic behind, it dashes up into foam, blue
diamonds it looks like, all along the rocks, like
ghosts playing at hide-and-seek." At Mablethorpe he saw " interminable waves rolling
along interminable shores of sand."

> Break, break, break,
>   On thy cold grey stones, O Sea !
> And I would that my tongue could utter
>   The thoughts that arise in me.
>
> O well for the fisherman's boy,
>   That he shouts with his sister at play !
> O well for the sailor lad,
>   That he sings in his boat on the bay !
>
> And the stately ships go on
>   To their haven under the hill ;
> But O for the touch of a vanish'd hand,
>   And the sound of a voice that is still !
>
> Break, break, break,
>   At the foot of thy crags, O Sea !
> But the tender grace of a day that is dead
>   Will never come back to me.

Finally, as we have seen, Tennyson now first
gave expression to that vision which haunted

him during the greater part of his long life—the dream of the Round Table. Like his own Everard, maybe, he had already written

> His Epic, his King Arthur, some twelve books

and burnt them.

> For nature brings not back the mastodon,
> Nor we those times,—and why should any man
> Remodel models ?

However it be, his riper judgment reversed this dictum, and the " Morte d'Arthur " remains a noble prelude to that great series of narratives, approaching the epic, in which the poet's message to mankind may be read, perhaps, in its fullest and most characteristic form. In the same volumes appeared " Sir Galahad " (foreshadowing " The Holy Grail ") and that beautiful fragment of

SIR LAUNCELOT AND QUEEN GUINEVERE

> Like souls that balance joy and pain,
> With tears and smiles from heaven again
> The maiden Spring upon the plain
> Came in a sun-lit fall of rain.
>   In crystal vapour everywhere
> Blue isles of heaven laugh'd between,
> And, far in forest-deeps unseen,
> The topmost elm-tree gather'd green
>   From draughts of balmy air.

Sometimes the linnet piped his song :
Sometimes the throstle whistled strong :
Sometimes the sparhawk, wheel'd along,
Hush'd all the groves from fear of wrong :
   By grassy capes with fuller sound
In curves the yellowing river ran,
And drooping chestnut-buds began
To spread into the perfect fan,
    Above the teeming ground.

Then, in the boyhood of the year,
Sir Launcelot and Queen Guinevere
Rode thro' the coverts of the deer,
With blissful treble ringing clear.
   She seem'd a part of joyous Spring :
A gown of grass-green silk she wore,
Buckled with golden clasps before ;
A light-green tuft of plumes she bore
    Closed in a golden ring.

Now on some twisted ivy-net,
Now by some tinkling rivulet,
In mosses mixt with violet
Her cream-white mule his pastern set :
   And fleeter now she skimm'd the plains
Than she whose elfin prancer springs
By night to eery warblings,
When all the glimmering moorland rings
    With jingling bridle-reins.

As she fled fast thro' sun and shade,
The happy winds upon her play'd,
Blowing the ringlet from the braid :
She look'd so lovely as she sway'd
   The rein with dainty finger-tips,

A man had given all other bliss,
And all his worldly worth for this,
To waste his whole heart in one kiss
Upon her perfect lips.

V

JUST a year after the 1842 "Poems" reached their fourth edition appeared "The Princess: A Medley" (1847), Tennyson's first long poem, and "after all one of the very finest studies of some social tendencies and phenomena which poet has ever wrought." It is curious to reflect that the beautiful songs, which Tennyson considered "the best interpreters of the poem," were not included until the third edition (1850); or the "weird seizures" of the Prince (revealing "his too emotional temperament and intended to emphasize his comparative want of power"), until the fourth (1851).

"The Princess" has been freely criticized, with satirical condescension, for its apparent frivolity in the treatment of a serious subject. Undoubtedly his "College," with mine host's daughter and housemaid for boys, has no very close resemblance to institutions with which we are now familiar; and the "conversion" of the Princess to conventionality may be called naive and rudimentary. Nevertheless the poet expresses herein his "strongest convictions of the true relation between men and women" which embody his whole philosophy of life. He fore-

38

saw the noble struggle of women for higher
education, declaring that "the sooner woman
finds out that she is 'not undevelopt man, but
diverse,' the better it will be for the progress of
the world."

> Let . . . this proud watchword rest
> Of equal ; seeing either sex alone
> Is half itself, and in true marriage lies
> Nor equal, nor unequal : each fulfils
> Defect in each, and always thought in thought,
> Purpose in purpose, will in will, they grow,
> The single pure and perfect animal,
> The two-cell'd heart beating, with one full stroke,
> Life.

And, moreover, for all his smooth playfulness,
the poet gives almost violent expression to the
eternal opposition of attitudes which lie at the
root of all so-called "woman" questions. "Take,
break her," cries the father of his Princess to
her lover :

> Boy,
> The bearing and the training of a child
> Is woman's wisdom.

With what keen irony he frames the obstinate
convictions of those upholding the old formulæ :

> Man is the hunter ; woman is his game :
> The sleek and shining creatures of the chase,
> We hunt them for the beauty of their skins ;
> They love us for it, and we ride them down.
> Wheedling and siding with them !

39

With what burning eloquence he " unfurls the
maiden banner of their rights," against what
" six thousand years " have " made them—
toys of men " :

> No wiser than their mothers, household stuff,
> Live chattels, mincers of each other's fame,
> Full of weak poison, turnspits for the clown,
> The drunkard's football, laughing-stocks of
>   Time,
> Whose brains are in their hands and in their
>   heels,
> But fit to flaunt, to dress, to dance, to thrum,
> To tramp, to scream, to burnish, and to scour,
> For ever slaves at home and fools abroad.

It is for them he claims the great gift, more
" breadth of culture."

> They worth it ? truer to the law within ?
> Severer in the logic of a life ?
> Twice as magnetic to sweet influences
> Of earth and heaven ?

In her appointed place she yet " stays all the
fair young planet in her hands," with space to

> Burgeon out of all
> Within her—let her make herself her own
> To give or keep, to live and learn and be
> All that not harms distinctive womanhood.

Finally for man the knightly ideal of " chivalrous reverence " :

> To love one maiden only, cleave to her,
> And worship her by years of noble deeds,
> Until they win her ; for indeed I know

> Of no more subtle master under heaven
> Than is the maiden passion for a maid,
> Not only to keep down the base in man,
> But teach high thought and amiable words,
> And courtliness and desire of fame,
> And love of truth, and all that makes a man.

Tennyson has told us that he " put songs between the separate divisions of the poem " because " the public did not see the drift. . . . The child is the link thro' the parts as shown in the songs." Charles Kingsley expounded their meaning :

" At the end of the first canto, fresh from the description of the female college, with its professoresses, and hostleresses, and other Utopian monsters, we turn the page, and—

> As through the land at eve we went.
>
> .   .   .   .   .
>
> O there above the little grave,
>   We kissed again with tears.

Between the next two cantos intervenes the well-known cradle-song, perhaps the best of all ; and at the next interval is the equally well-known bugle-song, the idea of which is twin-labour and twin-fame in a pair of lovers. In the next the memory of wife and child inspirits the soldier on the field ; in the next the sight of the fallen hero's child opens the sluices of his widow's tears ; and in the last . . . the poet has succeeded in superadding a new form of emotion to a canto in which he seemed to have exhausted every resource of pathos which his subject allowed.''

Ask me no more : the moon may draw the sea ;
  The cloud may stoop from heaven and take the
     shape,
  With fold to fold, of mountain or of cape ;
But O too fond, when have I answer'd thee ?
          Ask me no more.

Ask me no more : what answer should I give ?
  I love not hollow cheek or faded eye :
  Yet, O my friend, I will not have thee die !
Ask me no more, lest I should bid thee live ;
          Ask me no more.

Ask me no more : thy fate and mine are seal'd :
  I strove against the stream and all in vain :
  Let the great river take me to the main :
No more, dear love, for at a touch I yield ;
          Ask me no more.

Tennyson considered '' some of the blank verse in this poem among the best he ever wrote '' ; choosing such passages as :

Not peace she look'd—the Head : but rising up
Robed in the long night of her deep hair, so
To the open window moved, remaining there
Fixt like a beacon-tower above the waves
Of tempest, when the crimson rolling eye
Glares ruin, and the wild birds on the light
Dash themselves dead.   She stretch'd her arms
    and call'd
Across the tumult and the tumult fell.

TENNYSON & HIS POETRY

Or his description of a storm seen from
Snowdon :

> As one that climbs a peak to gaze
> O'er land and main, and sees a great black cloud
> Drag inward from the deeps, a wall of night,
> Blot out the slope of sea from verge to shore,
> And suck the blinding splendour from the sand,
> And quenching lake by lake, and tarn by tarn,
> Expunge the world.

"Tears, idle Tears," a "blank verse lyric,"
was written in the autumn at Tintern Abbey ;
and the poet considered his "Come down, O
maid, from yonder mountain height" (inspired
by Lauterbrunnen and Grindelwald) amongst
"his most successful work—for simple rhythm
and vowel music."

Perhaps the concluding dialogue may best
serve at once to summarize the philosophy of
the poem and illustrate the poet's power at this
period :

> "If you be, what I think you, some sweet dream,
> I would but ask you to fulfil yourself :
> But if you be that Ida whom I knew,
> I ask you nothing : only, if a dream,
> Sweet dream, be perfect. I shall die to-night.
> Stoop down and seem to kiss me ere I die."

> I could no more, but lay like one in trance,
> That hears his burial talk'd of by his friends,
> And cannot speak, nor move, nor make one sign,
> But lies and dreads his doom. She turn'd ; she
> paused ;

She stoop'd ; and out of languor leapt a cry ;
Leapt fiery Passion from the brinks of death ;
And I believed that in the living world
My spirit closed with Ida's at the lips ;
Till back I fell, and from mine arms she rose
Glowing all over noble shame ; and all
Her falser self slipt from her like a robe,
And left her woman, lovelier in her mood
Than in her mould that other, when she came
From barren deeps to conquer all with love ;
And down the streaming crystal dropt ; and she
Far-fleeted by the purple island-sides,
Naked, a double light in air and wave,
To meet her Graces, where they deck'd her out
For worship without end ; nor end of mine,
Stateliest, for thee ! but mute she glided forth,
Nor glanced behind her, and I sank and slept,
Fill'd thro' and thro' with Love, a happy sleep.

Deep in the night I woke : she, near me, held
A volume of the Poets of her land :
There to herself, all in low tones, she read.

'' Now sleeps the crimson petal, now the white ;
Nor waves the cypress in the palace walk ;
Nor winks the gold fin in the porphyry font :
The fire-fly wakens : waken thou with me.

Now droops the milkwhite peacock like a ghost,
And like a ghost she glimmers on to me.

Now lies the Earth all Danaë to the stars,
And all thy heart lies open unto me.

Now slides the silent meteor on, and leaves
A shining furrow, as thy thoughts in me.

Now folds the lily all her sweetness up,
And slips into the bosom of the lake :
So fold thyself, my dearest, thou, and slip
Into my bosom and be lost in me.''

I heard her turn the page ; she found a small
Sweet Idyl, and once more, as low, she read :

"Come down, O maid, from yonder mountain
    height :
What pleasure lives in height (the shepherd sang)
In height and cold, the splendour of the hills ?
But cease to move so near the Heavens, and cease
To glide a sunbeam by the blasted Pine,
To sit a star upon the sparkling spire ;
And come, for Love is of the valley, come,
For Love is of the valley, come thou down
And find him ; by the happy threshold, he,
Or hand in hand with Plenty in the maize,
Or red with spirted purple of the vats,
Or foxlike in the vine ; nor cares to walk
With Death and Morning on the Silver Horns,
Nor wilt thou snare him in the white ravine,
Nor find him dropt upon the firths of ice,
That huddling slant in furrow-cloven falls
To roll the torrent out of dusky doors :
But follow ; let the torrent dance thee down
To find him in the valley ; let the wild
Lean-headed Eagles yelp alone, and leave
The monstrous ledges there to slope, and spill
Their thousand wreaths of dangling water-smoke,
That like a broken purpose waste in air :
So waste not thou ; but come ; for all the vales
Await thee ; azure pillars of the hearth
Arise to thee ; the children call, and I
Thy shepherd pipe, and sweet is every sound,
Sweeter thy voice, but every sound is sweet ;

Myriads of rivulets hurrying thro' the lawn,
The moan of doves in immemorial elms,
And murmuring of innumerable bees.''

So she low-toned ; while with shut eyes I lay
Listening ; then look'd. Pale was the perfect face ;
The bosom with long sighs labour'd ; and meek
Seem'd the full lips, and mild the luminous eyes,
And the voice trembled and the hand. She said
Brokenly, that she knew it, she had fail'd
In sweet humility ; had fail'd in all ;
That all her labour was but as a block
Left in the quarry ; but she still were loth,
She still were loth to yield herself to one,
That wholly scorn'd to help their equal rights
Against the sons of men, and barbarous laws.
She pray'd me not to judge their cause from her
That wrong'd it, sought far less for truth than power
In knowledge : something wild within her breast,
A greater than all knowledge, beat her down.
And she had nursed me there from week to week :
Much had she learnt in little time. In part
It was ill counsel had misled the girl
To vex true hearts : yet was she but a girl—
'' Ah fool, and made myself a Queen of farce !
When comes another such ? never, I think,
Till the Sun drop dead from the signs.''
                                        Her voice
Choked, and her forehead sank upon her hands,
And her great heart thro' all the faultful Past
Went sorrowing in a pause I dared not break ;
Till notice of a change in the dark world
Was lispt about the acacias, and a bird,
That early woke to feed her little ones,
Sent from a dewy breast a cry for light :
She moved, and at her feet the volume fell.

TENNYSON & HIS POETRY

" Blame not thyself too much," I said, " nor blame
Too much the sons of men and barbarous laws ;
These were the rough ways of the world till now.
Henceforth thou hast a helper, me, that know
The woman's cause is man's : they rise or sink
Together, dwarf'd or godlike, bond or free :
For she that out of Lethe scales with man
The shining steps of Nature, shares with man
His nights, his days, moves with him to one goal,
Stays all the fair young planet in her hands—
If she be small, slight-natured, miserable,
How shall men grow ? but work no more alone !
Our place is much : as far as in us lies
We two will serve them both in aiding her—
Will clear away the parasitic forms
That seem to keep her up but drag her down—
Will leave her space to burgeon out of all
Within her—let her make herself her own
To give or keep, to live and learn and be
All that not harms distinctive womanhood.
For woman is not undevelopt man,
But diverse : could we make her as the man,
Sweet love were slain : his dearest bond is this,
Not like to like, but like in difference.
Yet in the long years liker must they grow ;
The man be more of woman, she of man ;
He gain in sweetness and in moral height,
Nor lose the wrestling thews that throw the world ;
She mental breadth, nor fail in childward care,
Nor lose the childlike in the larger mind ;
Till at the last she set herself to man,
Like perfect music unto noble words ;
And so these twain, upon the skirts of Time,
Sit side by side, full-summ'd in all their powers,

Dispensing harvest, sowing the To-be,
Self-reverent each and reverencing each,
Distinct in individualities,
But like each other ev'n as those who love.
Then comes the statelier Eden back to men :
Then reign the world's great bridals, chaste and calm :
Then springs the crowning race of humankind.
May these things be ! "

       Sighing she spoke : " I fear
They will not."

      " Dear, but let us type them now
In our own lives, and this proud watchword rest
Of equal ; seeing either sex alone
Is half itself, and in true marriage lies
Nor equal, nor unequal : each fulfils
Defect in each, and always thought in thought,
Purpose in purpose, will in will, they grow,
The single pure and perfect animal,
The two-cell'd heart beating, with one full stroke,
Life."

    And again sighing she spoke : " A dream
That once was mine ! what woman taught you this ? "

" Alone," I said, " from earlier than I know,
Immersed in rich foreshadowings of the world,
I loved the woman : he, that doth not, lives
A drowning life, besotted in sweet self,
Or pines in sad experience worse than death,
Or keeps his wing'd affections clipt with crime :
Yet was there one thro' whom I loved her, one
Not learned, save in gracious household ways,
Nor perfect, nay, but full of tender wants,
No Angel, but a dearer being, all dipt
In Angel instincts, breathing Paradise,
Interpreter between the Gods and men,
48

Who look'd all native to her place, and yet
On tiptoe seem'd to touch upon a sphere
Too gross to tread, and all male minds perforce
Sway'd to her from their orbits as they moved,
And girdled her with music.   Happy he
With such a mother ! faith in womankind
Beats with his blood, and trust in all things high
Comes easy to him, and tho' he trip and fall
He shall not blind his soul with clay.''

                                        '' But I,''
Said Ida, tremulously, '' so all unlike—
It seems you love to cheat yourself with words :
This mother is your model.   I have heard
Of your strange doubts : they well might be : I seem
A mockery to my own self.   Never, Prince ;
You cannot love me.''

                              '' Nay but thee,'' I said,
'' From yearlong poring on thy pictured eyes,
Ere seen I loved, and loved thee seen, and saw
Thee woman thro' the crust of iron moods
That mask'd thee from men's reverence up, and
        forced
Sweet love on pranks of saucy boyhood : now,
Giv'n back to life, to life indeed, thro' thee,
Indeed I love : the new day comes, the light
Dearer for night, as dearer thou for faults
Lived over : lift thine eyes ; my doubts are dead,
My haunting sense of hollow shows : the change,
This truthful change in thee has kill'd it.   Dear,
Look up, and let thy nature strike on mine,
Like yonder morning on the blind half-world ;
Approach and fear not ; breathe upon my brows ;
In that fine air I tremble, all the past
Melts mist-like into this bright hour, and this
Is morn to more, and all the rich to-come

Reels, as the golden Autumn woodland reels
Athwart the smoke of burning weeds. Forgive me,
I waste my heart in signs : let be. My bride,
My wife, my life. O we will walk this world,
Yoked in all exercise of noble end,
And so thro' those dark gates across the wild
That no man knows. Indeed I love thee : come,
Yield thyself up : my hopes and thine are one :
Accomplish thou my manhood and thyself ;
Lay thy sweet hands in mine and trust to me."

VI

MEANWHILE, at irregular intervals since
Hallam's death in 1833, Tennyson had
been writing in " a long butcher-ledger-
like book " those " Elegies " which became
" In Memoriam." They were spontaneous ex-
pressions of thought or emotion, originally
designed neither as one continuous poem nor for
publication. They contain little or no direct
revelation of Hallam's character ; no precise
record of a unique friendship. They form a
Philosophy of Life, founded on constant com-
munion with the dead : and when questioned
on faith or dogma Tennyson would say always,
" I have given my belief in ' In Memoriam.' "

Here faith " has the last word." Tennyson,
as we have said, had a profound interest in the
progress of science. " His general acceptance
of the scientific view is real and sincere,"
dominating his thoughts about Nature which
Wordsworth knew only " by simple observation

and interpreted by religious and sympathetic intuition.'' It was this fact which lent weight to his message, emphatically so for his own generation. Whether eagerly concerned with the minor differences, then temporarily prominent, between Theism and Christianity, or groping blindly among the great issues between agnosticism and faith, wise men recognized immediately his '' unparalleled combination of intensity of feeling with comprehensiveness of view and balance of judgment, shown in presenting the *deepest* needs and perplexities of humanity.'' Ever docile to the lessons of science, amid a grim '' fight with Death,'' Tennyson yet gives us God and Immortality, '' the indestructible and inalienable minimum of faith which humanity (the ' man in men ') cannot give up because it is necessary to life,'' because '' the man in us is deeper than the methodical thinker.''

> If e'er when faith had fall'n asleep,
>   I heard a voice, '' believe no more,''
>   And heard an ever-breaking shore
> That tumbled in the Godless deep ;
>
> A warmth within the breast would melt
>   The freezing reason's colder part,
>   And like a man in wrath the heart
> Stood up and answer'd '' I have felt.''
>
> No, like a child in doubt and fear :
>   But that blind clamour made me wise ;
>   Then was I as a child that cries,
> But, crying, knows his father near ;

And what I am beheld again
  What is, and no man understands ;
  And out of darkness came the hands
That reach thro' nature moulding men.

Westcott was most impressed by his " splendid
faith in the growing purpose of the sum of life,
and in the noble destiny of the individual man
as he offers himself for the fulfilment of his
little part."

LIII

Oh yet we trust that somehow good
  Will be the final goal of ill,
  To pangs of nature, sins of will,
Defects of doubt, and taints of blood :

That nothing walks with aimless feet :
  That not one life shall be destroy'd,
  Or cast as rubbish to the void,
When God hath made the pile complete ;

That not a worm is cloven in vain ;
  That not a moth with vain desire
  Is shrivel'd in a fruitless fire,
Or but subserves another's gain.

Behold, we know not anything ;
  I can but trust that good shall fall
  At last—far off—at last, to all,
And every winter change to spring.

So runs my dream : but what am I ?
  An infant crying in the night :
  An infant crying for the light :
And with no language but a cry.

LXXX

Could I have said while he was here
   " My love shall now no further range ;
   There cannot come a mellower change,
For now is love mature in ear."

Love, then, had hope of richer store :
   What end is here to my complaint ?
   This haunting whisper makes me faint,
" More years had made me love thee more."

But Death returns an answer sweet :
   " My sudden frost was sudden gain,
   And gave all ripeness to the grain,
It might have drawn from after-heat."

LXXI

Risest thou thus, dim dawn, again,
   And howlest, issuing out of night,
   With blasts that blow the poplar white,
And lash with storm the streaming pane ?

Day, when my crown'd estate begun
   To pine in that reverse of doom,
   Which sicken'd every living bloom,
And blurr'd the splendour of the sun ;

Who usherest in the dolorous hour
   With thy quick tears that make the rose
   Pull sideways, and the daisy close
Her crimson fringes to the shower ;

Who might'st have heaved a windless flame
   Up the deep East, or, whispering, play'd
   A chequer-work of beam and shade
From hill to hill, yet look'd the same,

53

As wan, as chill, as wild as now ;
   Day, mark'd as with some hideous crime,
   When the dark hand struck down thro' time,
And cancell'd nature's best : but thou,

Lift as thou may'st thy burthen'd brows
   Thro' clouds that drench the morning star,
   And whirl the ungarner'd sheaf afar,
And sow the sky with flying boughs,

And up thy vault with roaring sound
   Climb thy thick noon, disastrous day ;
   Touch thy dull goal of joyless grey,
And hide thy shame beneath the ground.

CXXX

O living will that shalt endure
   When all that seems shall suffer shock,
   Rise in the spiritual rock,
Flow thro' our deeds and make them pure,

That we may lift from out of dust
   A voice as unto him that hears,
   A cry above the conquer'd years
To one that with us works, and trust,

With faith that comes of self-control,
   The truths that never can be proved
   Until we close with all we loved,
And all we flow from, soul in soul.

The Introduction appears " to be the mature summing up after an interval of the many strains of thought in the Elegies " :

Strong Son of God, immortal Love,
    Whom we, that have not seen thy face
    By faith, and faith alone, embrace,
Believing where we cannot prove ;

Thine are these orbs of light and shade ;
    Thou madest Life in man and brute ;
    Thou madest Death ; and lo, thy foot
Is on the skull which thou hast made.

Thou wilt not leave us in the dust :
    Thou madest man, he knows not why ;
    He thinks he was not made to die ;
And thou hast made him : thou art just.

Thou seemest human and divine,
    The highest, holiest manhood, thou :
    Our wills are ours, we know not how ;
Our wills are ours, to make them thine.

Our little systems have their day ;
    They have their day and cease to be :
    They are but broken lights of thee,
And thou, O Lord, art more than they.

We have but faith : we cannot know ;
    For knowledge is of things we see ;
    And yet we trust it comes from thee,
A beam in darkness ; let it grow.

Let knowledge grow from more to more,
    But more of reverence in us dwell ;
    That mind and soul, according well,
May make one music as before,

55

But vaster. We are fools and slight ;
　　We mock thee when we do not fear :
　　But help thy foolish ones to bear ;
Help thy vain worlds to bear thy light.

Forgive what seem'd my sin in me ;
　　What seem'd my worth since I began ;
　　For merit lives from man to man,
And not from man, O Lord, to thee.

Forgive my grief for one removed,
　　Thy creature, whom I found so fair.
　　I trust he lives in thee, and there
I find him worthier to be loved.

Forgive these wild and wandering cries,
　　Confusions of a wasted youth ;
　　Forgive them where they fail in truth,
And in thy wisdom make me wise.

" Faith must give the last word : but the last
word," as Henry Sidgwick put it, " is not the
whole utterance of the truth ; the whole truth
is that assurance and doubt must alternate in
the moral world in which we at present live,
somewhat as night and day alternate in the
physical world. The revealing visions come and
go ; when they come we feel that we know ;
but in the intervals we must pass through states
in which all is dark, and in which we can only
struggle to hold the conviction that

　　Power is with us in the night
　　Which makes the darkness and the light
　　And dwells not in the light alone."

"In Memoriam" is "founded on friendship"; and, in addition to the deeper mysteries of faith, reveals much of Tennyson's ideal of the English gentleman, afterwards amplified in the "Idylls." One need not, therefore, criticize the poet for extravagance in judgment, since he says expressly "this is a poem, *not* an actual biography . . . the different moods of sorrow as in a drama are dramatically given."

By allusion rather than actual description the character, beloved and honoured, emerges the transfigured knight :

> My love has talk'd with rocks and trees ;
> He finds on misty mountain ground
> His own vast shadow glory-crown'd.
> He sees himself in all he sees.

Tennyson's knight has the visionary single-mindedness of a Sir Galahad, the natural possession of youth ; already mingled with the common-sense alertness toward a practical present, which gradually weaned him from his recurrent dreams of the Middle Ages. A good sportsman—as we have it to-day—a hard fighter and a hearty lover: with a certain spiritual intellectuality, breeding gentleness of manner, not always associated with the British type, a gentleman more of God than of man: while Tennyson was absorbed over "In Memoriam," it was inevitably this side of his personality which claimed most thought and expression. The friends loved bravery and enterprise, without having great occasion for exercising it :

they honoured liberty as inheritors of freedom :
their achievement was in the main as yet no
more than resolute determination. Heroes by
sympathy and intuition—unproven of life.

Philosophically, Tennyson was always academic—though capable of deeper and wider emotion than the pure scholar—and was stirred at this
time by past humanity. It is the dead Hallam
who sets him dreaming, and he dreams back-
ward, though never idly. Because honour was
a living power in him, purity a real force, his
words have a true meaning.

And so, as the problems of life—never shirked
or faced with indifference—crowded about him,
we shall find more and more in his work ; the
application of Idealism to fact, the recognition
of poetical beauty in the daily round, the heroism
of the average man. He never belittled ordinary
people ; and learnt, as the years passed, to read
God everywhere.

> O true and tried, so well and long,
>   Demand not thou a marriage lay ;
>   In that it is thy marriage day
> Is music more than any song.
>
> Nor have I felt so much of bliss
>   Since first he told me that he loved
>   A daughter of our house ; nor proved
> Since that dark day a day like this ;
>
> Tho' I since then have number'd o'er
>   Some thrice three years : they went and came
>   Remade the blood and changed the frame,
> And yet is love not less, but more ;

No longer caring to embalm
 In dying songs a dead regret,
 But like a statue solid-set,
And moulded in colossal calm.

Regret is dead, but love is more
 Than in the summers that are flown,
 For I myself with these have grown
To something greater than before ;

Which makes appear the songs I made
 As echoes out of weaker times,
 As half but idle brawling rhymes,
The sport of random sun and shade.

But where is she, the bridal flower,
 That must be made a wife ere noon ?
 She enters, glowing like the moon
Of Eden on its bridal bower :

On me she bends her blissful eyes
 And then on thee ; they meet thy look
 And brighten like the star that shook
Betwixt the palms of paradise.

O when her life was yet in bud,
 He too foretold the perfect rose.
 For thee she grew, for thee she grows
For ever, and as fair as good.

And thou art worthy ; full of power ;
 As gentle ; liberal-minded, great,
 Consistent ; wearing all that weight
Of learning lightly like a flower.

But now set out : the noon is near,
 And I must give away the bride ;
 She fears not, or with thee beside
And me behind her, will not fear :

For I that danced her on my knee,
    That watch'd her on her nurse's arm,
    That shielded all her life from harm
At last must part with her to thee ;

Now waiting to be made a wife,
    Her feet, my darling, on the dead ;
    Their pensive tablets round her head,
And the most living words of life

Breathed in her ear. The ring is on,
    The " wilt thou " answer'd, and again
    The " wilt thou " ask'd, till out of twain
Her sweet " I will " has made ye one.

Now sign your names, which shall be read,
    Mute symbols of a joyful morn,
    By village eyes as yet unborn ;
The names are sign'd, and overhead

Begins the clash and clang that tells
    The joy to every wandering breeze ;
    The blind wall rocks, and on the trees
The dead leaf trembles to the bells.

O happy hour, and happier hours
    Await them. Many a merry face
    Salutes them—maidens of the place,
That pelt us in the porch with flowers.

O happy hour, behold the bride
    With him to whom her hand I gave.
    They leave the porch, they pass the grave
That has to-day its sunny side.

To-day the grave is bright for me,
    For them the light of life increased,
    Who stay to share the morning feast,
Who rest to-night beside the sea.

Let all my genial spirits advance
 To meet and greet a whiter sun ;
 My drooping memory will not shun
The foaming grape of eastern France.

It circles round, and fancy plays,
 And hearts are warm'd and faces bloom,
 As drinking health to bride and groom
We wish them store of happy days.

Nor count me all to blame if I
 Conjecture of a stiller guest,
 Perchance, perchance, among the rest,
And, tho' in silence, wishing joy.

But they must go, the time draws on,
 And those white-favour'd horses wait ;
 They rise, but linger ; it is late ;
Farewell, we kiss, and they are gone.

A shade falls on us like the dark
 From little cloudlets on the grass,
 But sweeps away as out we pass
To range the woods, to roam the park,

Discussing how their courtship grew,
 And talk of others that are wed,
 And how she look'd, and what he said,
And back we come at fall of dew.

Again the feast, the speech, the glee,
 The shade of passing thought, the wealth
 Of words and wit, the double health,
The crowning cup, the three-times-three,

And last the dance ; —till I retire :
 Dumb is that tower which spake so loud,
 And high in heaven the streaming cloud,
And on the downs a rising fire :

61

And rise, O moon, from yonder down,
 Till over down and over dale
 All night the shining vapour sail
And pass the silent-lighted town,

The white-faced halls, the glancing rills,
 And catch at every mountain head,
 And o'er the friths that branch and spread
Their sleeping silver thro' the hills ;

And touch with shade the bridal doors,
 With tender gloom the roof, the wall ;
 And breaking let the splendour fall
To spangle all the happy shores

By which they rest, and ocean sounds,
 And, star and system rolling past,
 A soul shall draw from out the vast
And strike his being into bounds,

And, moved thro' life of lower phase,
 Result in man, be born and think,
 And act and love, a closer link
Betwixt us and the crowning race

Of those that, eye to eye, shall look
 On knowledge ; under whose command
 Is Earth and Earth's, and in their hand
Is Nature like an open book ;

No longer half-akin to brute,
 For all we thought and loved and did,
 And hoped, and suffer'd, is but seed
Of what in them is flower and fruit ;

Whereof the man, that with me trod
 This planet, was a noble type
 Appearing ere the times were ripe,
That friend of mine who lives in God

That God, which ever lives and loves,
One God, one law, one element,
And one far-off divine event,
To which the whole creation moves.

VII

TO a large extent, as we have seen, " In Memoriam " is Tennyson's answer to the riddle of the universe. It became, in another sense, the very practical solution of his personal life.

On his first meeting in the woods with Emily Sellwood, then aged seventeen, the poet cried out, " Are you a Dryad or an Oread wandering here ? " That was in 1830, and when, six years later, Charles Tennyson married her youngest sister Louisa, the fair bridesmaid touched his imagination more deeply. They were soon engaged, and the need of a " livelihood on which to marry " became an influence on his work and life. Three years' correspondence from 1838 to 1840 reveals much of his life ; and then any intercourse was forbidden ; though her mother had generously offered to divide her jointure with them that they might marry.

They waited ten years and then—Moxon offering a yearly royalty on " In Memoriam and the other poems "—their engagement was renewed, and in the same month (on June 13) they were married at Shiplake. Tennyson quaintly remarked that it was " the nicest wedding " he had ever been at—partly because the cake and dresses came " too late " : and added, in all seriousness, " the peace of God came into my life at the altar when I wedded her."

It was certainly a marked year, since in November he accepted the Laureateship, first offered to Rogers—strangely, it now would seem, because the Queen felt it necessary that the " office should be limited to a name bearing such distinction in the literary world as to do credit to the appointment."

One need not here dwell on private emotions beyond saying that Tennyson's anticipations from marriage were fully realized. The combination of quiet humour, tender spirituality and practical devotion, with an intellect of which he was proud, made her an almost ideal wife. She became the touchstone of all his work, being the one and only critic to whom the poems (already discussed and transcribed by her) were referred for final revision before publication.

In practical affairs they made a curious beginning, though afterwards becoming normal enough. After short occupations of houses lent by friends, they took a house in Warninglid, Sussex, which had attracted them by the airiness of the rooms and the view of the Downs : " The full song of the birds delighted us as we drove up to the door."

But when a storm had blown down part of their bedroom window, and investigations proved its association with a buried baby and a notorious gang of thieving murderers, the young couple beat a hasty retreat, Tennyson " drawing his wife in a bath-chair over a very rough road to Cuckfield." The next move was to Twickenham ; and in 1851, the year of the Great Exhibition, they took their first journey on the Continent, memorialized in " The Daisy," a picture of Italy " written at Edinburgh."

This metre—" a far-off echo of the Horatian alcaic "—was an invention of Tennyson's ; and reckoned, by himself, as one of his best. He practically repeated it, with a pleasing variation of the dactyl beginning at the fourth line of each verse, in the invitation to the Rev. F. D. Maurice (1854).

> Come, when no graver cares employ,
> Godfather, come and see your boy :
> Your presence will be sun in winter,
> Making the little one leap for joy.
>
> .　　.　　.　　.　　.
>
> Or later, pay one visit here,
> For there are few we hold as dear ;
> Nor pay but one, but come for many,
> Many and many a happy year.

Other inventions of which he was proud were "some of the anapæstic movements in 'Maud,'" and the swelling rhythm of the " Ode to Virgil." This period closes with the " Ode on the Death of the Duke of Wellington," which, curiously enough, was almost universally abused by the press ; though now we accept rather Henry Taylor's estimate of its " absolute simplicity and truth, with all the poetic passion of his nature moving beneath." It was published the morning of the funeral, November 1852 ; and similarly the immortal " Charge of the Light Brigade " was written in a few minutes " after reading the description in the ' Times ' in which occurred the phrase ' some one had blundered ' " —the origin of the metre of his poem.

VIII

THE " Little Hamlet," " Maud "—his " pet bantling "—has a very singular traditional origin. Accidentally rereading a poem of his own, published in a volume got up by Lord Northampton in aid of a sick clergyman, Tennyson felt, says Aubrey de Vere, " that, to render the poem fully intelligible, a preceding one was necessary. He wrote it ; the second poem, too, required a predecessor ; and thus the whole work was written, as it were, *backwards*." The responsible verses began with the now familiar " O that 'twere possible."

" All the people pronounced sardonic in this poem," said Tennyson, may be excused if one recognizes that " I do not cry out against the age as hopelessly bad, but try to point out where it is bad in order that each individual may do his best to redeem it ; as the evils I denounce are individual, only to be cured by each man looking to his own heart. I denounced evil in all its shapes, especially those considered venial by the world and society."

TENNYSON & HIS POETRY

That is the first duty of a young man ; and "Maud" is pre-eminently the voice of youth. Its somewhat disordered passion, wedded to lyrical outbursts of sheer music ; its eager reproaching and tender idealism ; its argumentativeness and its despair reflect the moods with which we are all familiar between the ages of eighteen and twenty-five. A cruel fate drove the hero to insanity (pronounced on medical authority to be "the most faithful representation of madness since Shakespeare") ; but for the most part his quarrel with the world is no less normal than his love for the one woman. Generous minds feel both kinds of emotion ; and if "Richard Feverell" contains, as R. L. Stevenson once noted, the most perfect picture of first love in English fiction, "Maud" has set the tune to music for all time. A dramatic setting, moreover, since—as the poet himself expressed it—the "different phases of passion in one person take the place of different characters."

The condensation of contemporary criticism in Dr. Mann's able "Maud Vindicated" is an instructive comment on the normal distrust of novelty. The favourite word used to describe the poem, from which indeed came the nickname of a school, was "spasm" ; others doubted whether "mud" or "mad" [1] were best applied to such outpourings. It was styled feverish, careless, rambling, obscure, "prose run mad" ; it revealed a "rampant and rabid blood-thirstiness

[1] Tennyson's first title was "Bared, or the Madness."

67

of soul " ; and one superior journalist discovered therein a " careless, visionary and
unreal allegory of the Russian War."

Every phrase reflects the normal attitude of
the Philistine toward earnest youth, combined
with an impatience of the need felt at the time,
even by friends like Gladstone, for " a good deal
of effort in order to comprehend it."

It is necessary, of course, to remember what
is supposed to have happened before the story
proper begins. The hero is already predisposed to
melancholy by long brooding on the sudden and
violent death of his father, following losses by
speculation, and possibly self-inflicted ; concerning which he suspects foul play somewhere,
" because an old friend of his family became
suddenly and unaccountably rich by the same
transaction that had brought ruin to the dead."

It is fairly obvious that the successful neigh-
bour will return as lord of the manor, and that
the hero will fall in love with his daughter, the
pet playmate of childhood :

Perfectly beautiful : let it be granted her : where is
    the fault ?
All that I saw (for her eyes were downcast, not to be
    seen)
Faultily faultless, icily regular, splendidly null,
Dead perfection, no more ; nothing more . . . .
Passionless, pale, cold face, star-sweet on a gloom
    profound.

That is a first impression, breeding curses on
wealth and the world ; but his mood changes,

passions awake, and we are led up to the duel with Maud's brother.

> Ah, wherefore cannot I be
> Like things of the season gay, like the bountiful
> season bland.

"Most of all," safe "from the cruel madness of love." Till the "chivalrous battle-song" she "warbled alone in her joy" stirs longings :

XI

> O let the solid ground
>   Not fail beneath my feet
> Before my life has found
>   What some have found so sweet ;
> Then let come what come may,
> What matter if I go mad,
> I shall have had my day.
>
> Let the sweet heavens endure,
>   Not close and darken above me
> Before I am quite quite sure
>   That there is one to love me ;
> Then let come what come may
> To a life that has been so sad,
> I shall have had my day.

And at last, discovering the wonder of her answering passion, the poet exults :

XVII

> Go not, happy day,
>   From the shining fields,
> Go not, happy day,
>   Till the maiden yields.

69

Rosy is the West,
　　Rosy is the South,
Roses are her cheeks,
　　And a rose her mouth.
When the happy Yes
　　Falters from her lips,
Pass and blush the news
　　O'er the blowing ships.
Over blowing seas,
　　Over seas at rest,
Pass the happy news,
　　Blush it thro' the West ;
Till the red man dance
　　By his red cedar tree,
And the red man's babe
　　Leap, beyond the sea.
Blush from West to East,
　　Blush from East to West,
Till the West is East,
　　Blush it thro' the West.
Rosy is the West,
　　Rosy is the South,
Roses are her cheeks,
　　And a rose her mouth.

" There is none like her, none " ! And it is
now, in confidence, he calls :

XXII

Come into the garden, Maud,
　　For the black bat, night, has flown,
Come into the garden, Maud,
　　I am here at the gate alone ;
And the woodbine spices are wafted abroad,
　　And the musk of the roses blown.

For a breeze of morning moves,
   And the planet of Love is on high,
Beginning to faint in the light that she loves
   On a bed of daffodil sky,
To faint in the light of the sun she loves,
   To faint in his light, and to die.

All night have the roses heard
   The flute, violin, bassoon ;
All night has the casement jessamine stirr'd
   To the dancers dancing in tune ;
Till a silence fell with the waking bird,
   And a hush with the setting moon.

I said to the lily, " There is but one
   With whom she has heart to be gay.
When will the dancers leave her alone ?
   She is weary of dance and play."
Now half to the setting moon are gone,
   And half to the rising day ;
Low on the sand and loud on the stone
   The last wheel echoes away.

I said to the rose, " The brief night goes
   In babble and revel and wine.
O young lord-lover, what sighs are those,
   For one that will never be thine ?
But mine, but mine," so I sware to the rose,
   " For ever and ever, mine."

And the soul of the rose went into my blood,
   As the music clash'd in the hall ;
And long by the garden lake I stood,
   For I heard your rivulet fall
From the lake to the meadow and on to the
     wood,
   Our wood, that is dearer than all ;

From the meadow your walks have left so sweet
   That whenever a March-wind sighs
He sets the jewel-print of your feet
   In violets blue as your eyes,
To the woody hollows in which we meet
   And the valleys of Paradise.

The slender acacia would not shake
   One long milk-bloom on the tree ;
The white lake-blossom fell into the lake,
   As the pimpernel dozed on the lea ;
But the rose was awake all night for your sake,
   Knowing your promise to me ;
The lilies and roses were all awake,
   They sigh'd for the dawn and thee.

Queen rose of the rosebud garden of girls,
   Come hither, the dances are done,
In gloss of satin and glimmer of pearls,
   Queen lily and rose in one ;
Shine out, little head, sunning over with curls,
   To the flowers, and be their sun.

There has fallen a splendid tear
   From the passion-flower at the gate.
She is coming, my dove, my dear ;
   She is coming, my life, my fate ;
The red rose cries, " She is near, she is near " ;
   And the white rose weeps, " She is late " ;
The larkspur listens, " I hear, I hear " ;
   And the lily whispers, " I wait."

She is coming, my own, my sweet ;
   Were it ever so airy a tread,
My heart would hear her and beat,
   Were it earth in an earthy bed ;

My dust would hear her and beat,
　　Had I lain for a century dead ;
Would start and tremble under her feet,
　　And blossom in purple and red.

After the duel comes Part II, when, crying "the fault was mine," he sits "stunn'd and still," with guilty hand " plucking the harmless wild-flower." Travel is powerless to stay the o'er-whelming of reason. Death comes to the release of Maud, and to him nothing save prayer for yet deeper burial.

XXVII

Dead, long dead,
Long dead !
And my heart is a handful of dust,
And the wheels go over my head,
And my bones are shaken with pain,
For into a shallow grave they are thrust,
Only a yard beneath the street,
And the hoofs of the horses beat, beat,
The hoofs of the horses beat,
Beat into my scalp and my brain,
With never an end to the stream of passing feet,
Driving, hurrying, marrying, burying,
Clamour and rumble, and ringing and clatter,
And here beneath it is all as bad,
For I thought the dead had peace, but it is not so ;
To have no peace in the grave, is that not sad ?
But up and down and to and fro,
Ever about me the dead men go ;
And then to hear a dead man chatter
Is enough to drive one mad.

Wretchedest age, since Time began,
They cannot even bury a man ;

73

And tho' we paid our tithes in the days that are
    gone
Not a bell was rung, not a prayer was read ;
It is that which makes us loud in the world of the
    dead ;
There is none that does his work, not one ;
A touch of their office might have sufficed,
But the churchmen fain would kill their church,
As the churches have kill'd their Christ.

See, there is one of us sobbing,
No limit to his distress ;
And another, a lord of all things, praying
To his own great self, as I guess ;
And another, a statesman there, betraying
His party-secret, fool, to the press ;
And yonder a vile physician, blabbing
The case of his patient—all for what ?
To tickle the maggot born in an empty head,
And wheedle a world that loves him not,
For it is but a world of the dead.

Nothing but idiot gabble !
For the prophecy given of old
And then not understood,
Has come to pass as foretold ;
Not let any man think for the public good,
But babble, merely for babble.
For I never whisper'd a private affair
Within the hearing of cat or mouse,
No, not to myself in the closet alone,
But I heard it shouted at once from the top of the
    house ;
Everything came to be known :
Who told *him* we were there ?

Not that gray old wolf, for he came not back
From the wilderness, full of wolves, where he used to
    lie ;
He has gather'd the bones for his o'ergrown whelp to
    crack ;
Crack them now for yourself, and howl, and die.

Prophet, curse me the blabbing lip,
And curse me the British vermin, the rat ;
I know not whether he came in the Hanover ship,
But I know that he lies and listens mute
In an ancient mansion's crannies and holes :
Arsenic, arsenic, sure, would do it,
Except that now we poison our babes, poor souls !
It is all used up for that.

Tell him now : she is standing here at my head ;
Not beautiful now, not even kind ;
He may take her now ; for she never speaks her
    mind,
But is ever the one thing silent here.
She is not of us, as I divine ;
She comes from another stiller world of the dead,
Stiller, not fairer than mine.

But I know where a garden grows,
Fairer than aught in the world beside,
All made up of the lily and rose
That blow by night, when the season is good,
To the sound of dancing music and flutes :
It is only flowers, they had no fruits,
And I almost fear they are not roses, but blood ;
For the keeper was one, so full of pride,
He linkt a dead man there to a spectral bride ;
For he, if he had not been a Sultan of brutes,
Would he have that hole in his side ?

But what will the old man say ?
He laid a cruel snare in a pit
To catch a friend of mine one stormy day ;
Yet now I could even weep to think of it ;
For what will the old man say
When he comes to the second corpse in the pit ?

Friend, to be struck by the public foe,
Then to strike him and lay him low,
That were a public merit, far,
Whatever the Quaker holds, from sin ;
But the red life spilt for a private blow—
I swear to you, lawful and lawless war
Are scarcely even akin.

O me, why have they not buried me deep enough ?
Is it kind to have made me a grave so rough,
Me, that was never a quiet sleeper ?
Maybe still I am but half-dead ;
Then I cannot be wholly dumb ;
I will cry to the steps above my head,
And somebody, surely, some kind heart will come
To bury me, bury me
Deeper, ever so little deeper.

But Tennyson would not leave us in the corpse-haunted madhouse. His robust and genial imagination pictures recovery, however shattered, and a third part, " written when the cannon was heard booming from the battle-ships in the Solent before the Crimean War," tells of life once more awake to the higher aims, through " the blood-red blossom of war with a heart of fire."

76

Let it flame or fade, and the war roll down like a
    wind,
We have proved we have hearts in a cause, we are
    noble still,
And myself have waked, as it seems, to the better
    mind ;
It is better to fight for the good than to rail at the ill;
I have felt with my native land, I am one with my
    kind,
I embrace the purpose of God, and the doom assign'd.

The vigorous variety of metrical effects in
" Maud " is almost unique. Every mood has
its own measure : now the long sweep ringing
with fiery indignation ; anon the moaning of
solitary despair. On one page the tender-sweet
melancholy of love denied ; at another the very
triumph of confident passion. Invective, philosophy, and narrative alternate with some of the
most perfect lyrics in the language—of which,
by the way, Tennyson himself liked best, " I
have led her home " (Part I, Canto XVIII),
" O that 'twere possible " (Part II, Canto IV)
and

       Courage, poor heart of stone !
       I will not ask thee why
       Thou canst not understand
       That thou art left for ever alone :
       Courage, poor stupid heart of stone.—
       Or if I ask thee why,
       Care not thou to reply :
       She is but dead, and the time is at hand
       When thou shalt more than die.

IX

AS already indicated, Tennyson's life was externally uneventful; though he had a few intimate friends, genial comradeship with most "persons of importance" in his day, and enthusiasm for travel. We find him summarizing Swinburne as a "very modest and intelligent young fellow"; sitting to Watts for what his friends called "the great moonlight portrait"; constantly in talk with the Carlyles, Brownings, Gladstone, Ruskin, Thackeray and, generally, the salt of the earth. He has settled down to the accepted position of a great man; never indifferent to national or social happenings; but before all an artist, loving and labouring at his art.

And now we approach the Epic for which he had allowed himself twenty years and actually required forty—the Arthurian cycle. The ideal of "In Memoriam," variously clothed, remains the heart of his message to mankind. "I hope I have enough of the old-world loyalty left in me not to wear my lady's favours against all comers," he writes, while hesitating to accept a baronetcy: and for him the old-world is always with us.

He describes his epic as "the dream of man coming into practical life and ruined by one sin. Birth is a mystery and death is a mystery, and in the midst lies the tableland of life, and its struggles and performances. It is not the history of one man or of one generation, but of

TENNYSON & HIS POETRY

a whole cycle of generations." It is a history which shows progress and advance : cynicism, indifference, selfishness, and materialism proving powerless against one with his " sword bathed in heaven." It paints for us the unconquerable vigour of Hope ; the " marvellous transmuting power of repentance to all men " ; the great everlasting battle between Sense and Soul. As Fitzgerald once put it: " The whole myth of Arthur's Round Table Dynasty in Britain presents itself before me with a sort of cloudy, Stonehenge grandeur."

Tennyson was always making prose notes on Arthur : he made a poem " in his head," and forgot it, on Lancelot's quest of the San Graal : he carried the epic scheme in his mind for over thirty years. A memorandum, with quite other allegorical drift than afterwards adopted, the rough draft of a scenario for a masque, and other fragments were among his manuscripts of early date. The first published expression of his life-long dream came in the lyrical " Lady of Shalott " (1832), while the 1842 volume contained " The Morte d'Arthur," " Sir Galahad," and " Sir Launcelot and Queen Guinevere."

The ultimate form of the poem was determined in 1855, the first instalment—Enid, Vivien, Guinevere, and Elaine (another version of the " Lady of Shalott ")—appeared in 1859. Then came a pause. He did not feel that further work in this strain would be appropriate at the moment, and was in no mood for it : he fancied the ghost-like passing away of the King in

" Guinevere " as a close ; he feared the charge
of irreverence—of " playing with sacred things "
—in approaching the Grail : he doubted whether
he could keep up the level already attained, and
would avoid the risk of " failure and time lost."
It was after about ten years that " The Holy
Grail " came to him, as it were, suddenly,
appearing in 1869, with " The Coming of
Arthur," " Pelleas and Ettarre," and " The
Passing of Arthur " (absorbing the early
" Morte d'Arthur "). Another decade brought
" The Last Tournament," privately printed,
published in the " Contemporary " in 1871, and
with " Gareth and Lynette " in 1872. " Balin
and Balan " completed the twelve books (of his
Introduction to " Morte d'Arthur ") in 1885.

As originally conceived, King Arthur repre-
sents " religious faith " ; the Round Table,
" liberal institutions " ; Merlin, " science " ;
Modred, " the sceptical understanding " ; the
three Queens (of Arthur's last journey), " Faith,
Hope, Charity, and more." Camelot, here as
everywhere, symbolizes spiritual growth. " The
Coming of Arthur is on the night of the New
Year " ; at his marriage the world is white with
May ; the vision of the Holy Grail comes in
summer ; the Last Tournament and Guinevere's flight in " the yellowing autumn " ; the
passing of Arthur at midnight in midwinter.
Yet " there is no single fact or incident in the
' Idylls,' however seemingly mystical, which
cannot be explained as without any mystery or
allegory whatever " ; and " Poetry is like shot-

silk with many glancing colours.   Every reader
must find his own interpretation according to his
own ability, and according to his sympathy with
the poet."

Through every line we can read of the King's,
and the poet's, " ideal knight," so eloquently
summarized in the " Dedication " to the Prince
Consort, who seemed himself " scarce other " :

" Who reverenced his conscience as his king ;
Whose glory was, redressing human wrong ;
Who spake no slander, no, nor listen'd to it ;
Who loved one only and who clave to her—"
Her—over all whose realms to their last isle,
Commingled with the gloom of imminent war,
The shadow of His loss drew like eclipse,
Darkening the world.   We have lost him : he is gone :
We know him now : all narrow jealousies
Are silent ; and we see him as he moved,
How modest, kindly, all-accomplish'd, wise,
With what sublime repression of himself,
And in what limits, and how tenderly ;
Not swaying to this faction or to that ;
Not making his high place the lawless perch
Of wing'd ambitions, nor a vantage-ground
For pleasure ; but thro' all this tract of years
Wearing the white flower of a blameless life,
Before a thousand peering littlenesses,
In that fierce light which beats upon a throne,
And blackens every blot : for where is he,
Who dares foreshadow for an only son
A lovelier life, a more unstain'd, than his ? |
Or how should England dreaming of *his* sons
Hope more for these than some inheritance
Of such a life, a heart, a mind as thine,

> Thou noble Father of her Kings to be,
> Laborious for her people and her poor—
> Voice in the rich dawn of an ampler day—
> Far-sighted summoner of War and Waste
> To fruitful strifes and rivalries of peace—
> Sweet nature gilded by the gracious gleam
> Of letters, dear to Science, dear to Art,
> Dear to thy land and ours, a Prince indeed,
> Beyond all titles, and a household name,
> Hereafter, thro' all times, Albert the Good.

We find a legendary England—" great tracts of wilderness constantly prey to the heathen "—

> Wherein the beast was ever more and more,
> But man was less and less till Arthur came.

> .   .   .   .   .

> Who thro' the puissance of his Table Round,
> Drew all their petty princedoms under him,
> Their King and head ; and made a realm, and reign'd.

Supposed son of Uther and Ygerne, brought up by the sage Merlin, Arthur appears almost without warning or preparation, " crown'd on the dais," followed by knights, " few, but all brave, all of one mind with him " ; near his throne " three fair queens "—" sweet faces, who will help him at his need "—and the Lady of the Lake, " cloth'd in white samite, mystic, wonderful " :

> She gave the King his huge cross-hilt'd sword,
> Whereby to drive the heathen out.

He marries Guinevere, fair daughter of Leodogran ; refuses tribute to Rome ; " threw the

kings," and in " twelve great battles " set free
the land from invasion.

> The King will follow Christ, and we the King.

Then follow various Tales of the Table.
First Gareth, last tall son of Lot, "a yet warm
corpse, and yet unburiable," and Bellicent, the
too good mother : himself the type of eternal
youth : his quest to rescue the broken Soul
from Death.   Like his good mother, indeed, we
"hold him still a child," while "prison'd, and
kept and coax'd and whistled to," seeing " the
great Sun of Glory," he vows " to weary her
ears with one continuous prayer " : that he may
serve the King, " working his will to cleanse the
world."

> Live pure, speak true, right wrong, follow the King,
> Else wherefore born ?

She, fond woman, would rather " seek him out
some comfortable bride and fair " ; but yield-
ing, half in pity, half in craft, bids him first
" serve disguised " a twelvemonth and a day
among the scullions and the kitchen-knaves.
And the boy answers :

> The thrall in person may be free in soul,
> And I shall see the jousts.

In the morality of knighthood, indeed, it made
but a poor approach to Arthur, who could "not
brook the shadow of any lie " :

> Our one white lie sits like a little ghost
> Here on the threshold of our enterprise.

> Let love be blamed for it, not she, nor I :
> Well, we will make amends.

The generous youth will not allow himself even
in thought to reproach her wistful tenderness
for the shame put upon him, as full of hope and
courage he rides southward to Camelot.

>   The birds made
> Melody on branch, and melody in mid-air.
> The damp hill-slopes were quicken'd into green,
> And the live green had kindled into flowers,
> For it was past the time of Easterday.
>
>   .   .   .
>
> Far off they saw the silver-misty morn
> Rolling her smoke about the Royal mount,
> That rose between the forest and the field.
> At times the summit of the high city flash'd ;
> At times the spires and turrets half-way down
> Prick'd through the mist ; at times the great gate
>   shone
> Only, that open'd on the field below :
> Anon the whole fair city had disappear'd.

Till to the simple minds of his two companions
it seemed a veritable "city of Enchanters, built
by fairy kings."
  At last they reach the court, where the clash
of arms sounds good in Gareth's ears—

> And out of bower and casement shyly glanced
> Eyes of pure women, wholesome stars of love ;
> And all about a healthful people stept
> As in the presence of a gracious king.

Then, hearing many a boon wisely granted, Gareth, ashamed, proffers his need, and is handed to Seneschal Kay, with due warning from the courtly Lancelot. Kay, the sour-minded, will have none of Lancelot's "mysteries," and treats the boy rather the more harshly for his gentle ways. But not for long, since Bellicent, hearing of her son's good service so patiently suffered, sent arms and "loosed him from his vow." So, telling the king his secret, Gareth, praying his name and quality be still hidden, begs, and is granted, the first quest.

> Then that same day there past into the hall
> A damsel of high lineage and a brow
> May-blossom, and a cheek of apple-blossom,
> Hawk-eyes; and lightly was her slender nose
> Tip-tilted like the petal of a flower.

Like all who approached the good King she came seeking justice, freedom, and a knight to succour her. The message, indeed, was for Lancelot, the prince of knights, that he would do battle with four tyrannical brothers holding captive her sister Lyonors with a view to forcing her into marriage. Arthur, assuring her that his order lives to "crush all wrongers of the realm," yet remembers his promise to Gareth and grants him the quest.

Then follows one of the daintiest passages of idyllic comedy in the language. The proud Lynette will have none of his kitchen-knave, and, "ere a man in hall could stay her," turned and fled. Naturally, however, the young knight finds no difficulty in overtaking her, and one by one, despite much pretty jesting and holding of the nose for kitchen smells, overthrows her enemies ; winning respect for his ever-gentle courtesy and matchless courage.

> And he that told the tale in older times
> Says that Sir Gareth wedded Lyonors,
> But he that told it later, says Lynette.

Probably the peculiar charm of this Idyll is derived from the dialogues. The maid's scorning and her cavalier's patience are told in verse of rare simplicity and delicate music, which is almost childlike, yet reveals perfect mastery of art. The whole atmosphere is one of boyish adventure and girlish petulance, which only a heart kept young by purity could either conceive or carry out. We have here the ideal of chivalry in its most elementary and, perhaps, its most pleasing aspect.

The following Idyll, now printed as two, gives us the reverse side of a similar picture, since we have here the man ungentle and the woman forbearing. By an almost fiendish device Geraint commands silence from Enid while she, loving, risks his displeasure by warnings of hidden danger. There is much, again, in Yniol's daughter, suggesting the patient Griselda. Chaucer, reproving, yet proved the humility of perfect womanhood by even rougher tests than Tennyson attributes to his knight of chivalry. But the same ideal of unquestioning obedience pervades both poems ; and it is quite evident

86

none of the Round Table could even imagine
that a " good " woman might behave differently.
The right of a husband to test and taunt is taken
for granted ; the *duty* of a wife to obey.

Enid's character stands out sweet and self-
sacrificing from the beginning. In the house of
her old father, himself enduring much trouble,
Geraint found her in

> faded silk,
> A faded mantle and a faded veil,

intent on " lowly handmaid work."

> And Enid brought sweet cakes to make them cheer,
> And in her veil enfolded, manchet bread.
> And then, because their hall must also serve
> For kitchen, boil'd the flesh, and spread the board,
> And stood behind, and waited on the three.
> And seeing her so sweet and serviceable,
> Geraint had longing in him evermore
> To stoop and kiss the tender little thumb,
> That crost the trencher as she laid it down.

So waiting upon father and mother, she, any man
of the middle ages would think, must be wife
for him. And Geraint, naturally, having slain
Yniol's enemies, married his daughter. Then,
since she grew to be much loved by Guinevere,
now breathed upon by scandal, he came to
doubt her fidelity ; and, begging the King's
permission to leave the court in defence of his
own princedom, took home the too fair damsel :

> Where, thinking, that if ever yet was wife
> True to her lord, mine shall be so to me,
> He compass'd her with sweet observances

> And worship, never leaving her, and grew
> Forgetful of his promise to the King,
> Forgetful of the falcon and the hunt,
> Forgetful of the tilt and tournament,
> Forgetful of his glory and his name,
> Forgetful of his princedom and its cares.
> And this forgetfulness was hateful to her.

Since true knighthood meant love of adventure and hard knocks, the ever-present eagerness to be up and doing, "I cannot love my lord and not his name." Then seeking, characteristically, some fault in herself, Enid, pondering, by ill-chance on her supposed unworthiness, murmured one night over him the fatal words, "O me, I fear that I am no true wife."

The spark thus kindled, a journey follows curiously similar to that of Gareth and Lynette, yet different from it. Geraint drives Enid before him into the wilderness, wherein, daring his anger for disobedience, she warns him again and again of those who would take advantage of his mood ; yet always suffers in silence his most unmerited reproach.

> Attending her rough lord, tho' all unask'd,
> In silence, did him service as a squire.

Like Gareth, too, he conquers everywhere against long odds ; until at last, stirred by the rare union of dignity and meekness with which she bears her insults and sufferings, and moved
88

by her sweet tending of his well-earned wounds,
he cries aloud :

> Henceforward I will rather die than doubt.
>
> .   .   .   .   .
>
> And never yet, since high in Paradise
> O'er the four rivers the first roses blew,
> Came purer pleasure unto mortal kind
> Than lived thro' her, who in that perilous hour
> Put hand to hand beneath her husband's heart,
> And felt him hers again : she did not weep,
> But o'er her meek eyes came a happy mist,
> Like that which kept the heart of Eden green
> Before the useful trouble of the rain.

There is, moreover, a curious episode in
" Geraint and Enid " which stands outside the
main story and yet illustrates one of the central
morals of the whole " Idylls " : the possibility
of *genuine* repentance resulting in permanent
reformation.   Geraint's first tilt for Enid was
against her cousin Edyrn, named the Sparrow-
hawk, who " would have slain her father, seized
herself," and had, incidentally, insulted Guinevere.   Hence Geraint sends him to court with
an apology.

> Where first as sullen as a beast new-caged,
> And waiting to be treated like a wolf,
> Because I knew my deeds were known, I found,
> Instead of scornful pity or pure scorn,
> Such fine reserve and noble reticence,
> Manners so kind, yet stately, such a grace
> Of tenderest courtesy, that I began
> To glance behind me at my former life
> And find that it had been the wolf's indeed.

Arthur's own testimony to the effect is without reserve :

> His very face with change of heart is changed,
> The world will not believe a man repents :
> And this wise world of ours is mainly right,
> Full seldom doth a man repent, or use
> Both grace and will to pick the vicious quitch
> Of blood and custom wholly out of him,
> And make all clean, and plant himself afresh.
> Edyrn has done it, weeding all his heart
> As I will weed this land before I go.

We see here the King's own ambition ; and in the earlier passage the kind of influence and the manners by which the standard of the Round Table was created and maintained. The ideal of courtesy and reticence toward the villain of the piece somewhat modifies our usual conception of the mediæval. The introduction of such an incident, so complete in itself and so subtly woven into Enid's story, affords striking evidence of the care and art with which Tennyson worked out his picture of the period.

It is difficult, perhaps, to regard the afterthought of " Balin and Balan " as other than an outside episode ; though the story was evidently a favourite with Tennyson himself. The two brothers sit "statue-like to right and left the spring," challenging all passers-by, because one of them, surnamed " the Savage," had " smote upon the naked skull a thrall," thus proving himself unfit for gentle society. The story of their reinstallation at the court and curious unworldliness bred of solitude, of the sleeping fury of Balin's temperament not yet wholly tamed, and of their tragic end " together by one doom "—" death-drowsing either lock'd in either's arm "—is scarce a tale of chivalry, but rather of a brain turned by much thinking on the Ideal. Balin, at least, seems a type that could never rise to the King's dream of manhood ; and their story, if elevated by his own good blow, is yet shadowed by the great sin. An ill word spoken lightly of Guinevere fires the " mood " of Balin, and the siren Vivien completes his undoing.

Yet, if it carries us beneath and beyond the clear atmosphere of the earliest " Idylls," no less it prepares the way for what is inevitably to follow.

As the two first " Idylls " may fairly be said to embody the " youth " of chivalry, we find in " Merlin and Vivien " an entirely different atmosphere : that which hovers always round life with any beginning of civilization or organized attempt at reform. Vivien, closely, if temporarily, allied with the sinister jealousy of Mark, is the " face-flatterer " and backbiter who judges " all nature by her feet of clay."

> O true and tender ! O my liege and king !
> O selfless man and stainless gentleman,
> Who would'st against thine own eye-witness fain
> Have all men true and leal, all women pure ;
> How, in the mouths of base interpreters,
> From over-fineness not intelligible

> To things with every sense as false and foul
> As the poach'd filth that floods the middle street,
> Is thy white blamelessness accounted blame !

Forgetting caution, she had suffered her tongue to

> Rage like a fire among the noblest names,
> Polluting, and imputing her whole self,
> Declaiming and defacing, till she left
> Not even Lancelot brave, nor Galahad clean.

Hers is the attitude of one who, base himself, trusts no man. It is not the mere recognition of weakness in noble natures, a fact none questions, by which she poisons the mind, but her persistent discrediting of *every* good motive or high resolve. She and with her the crowd are one in this—

> That if they find
> Some stain or blemish in a name of note,
> Not grieving that their greatest are so small,
> Inflate themselves with some insane delight.

Her " whispering " spreads quickly from ear to ear, in direct opposition to chivalric ideals— " as Arthur in the highest leaven'd the world, so Vivien in the lowest." Some colour is lent to her insinuations by the actual scandal, then gathering credence, concerning Lancelot and Guinevere : from which comes the Tragedy of Arthur. Wherein, also, lay a strange danger of perverted idealism—as Merlin reads. Asked by Vivien whether their " fair example " is followed in " Arthur's household," he " answer'd innocently " :

> Ay, by some few—ay, truly—youths that hold
> It more beseems the perfect virgin knight
> To worship woman as true wife beyond
> All hopes of gaining, than as maiden girl.
> They place their pride in Lancelot and the Queen.
> So passionate for utter purity
> Beyond the limit of their bond, are these,
> For Arthur bound them not to singleness.
> Brave hearts and clean ! and yet—God guide them
> —young.

Actually, the Idyll is mainly concerned with Vivien's crafty subjugation of Merlin, the wise foster-father to the King and sole repository of the true mystery in his birth. Foiled and flouted by younger men, she plies the sage with arts subtly contrasted with the maidenly love-making of Enid or Lynette. As " seeming-injured, simple-hearted thing " or as " a virtuous gentlewoman deeply wronged," she coaxes from him

> The charm
> Of woven paces and of waving hands,

whereby, leaving him as dead, she may work much mischief and secure revenge against the virtue that will have none of her.

In " Lancelot and Elaine " we learn more of the food on which such as Vivien flourish. The most perfect knight of the Round Table, " a man made to be loved," must die " a lonely

93

man, wifeless and heirless," a warning to all posterity, because of his sin. Best friend to the King, lover to his wife, is Lancelot. The Idyll tells us of what might have been. Chance leads the knight to Astolat and the " lily maid." Elaine, " sweet and serviceable," like Enid, is already a dreamer.

> Then the great knight, the darling of the court,
> Loved of the loveliest, into that rude hall
> Swept with all grace, and not with half disdain
> Hid under grace, as in a smaller time,
> But kindly man moving among his kind :
> Whom they with meats and vintage of their
>   best,
> And talk and minstrel melody entertain'd.

His " severe melancholy," broken with " sudden beaming tenderness of manners and of nature," weaves a spell her simple heart is powerless to escape.

> And all night long his face before her lived . . .
> Dark-splendid, speaking in the silence, full
> Of noble things, and held her from her sleep.

Though her elder by some score of years, Lancelot was the man of all men most inevitably to charm a hero-worshipper bred far from courts and ever pondering over great deeds. The talk of father and brother would but feed her fancy : and when fate led her to watch over his shield, to lend him her favour and, finally, to nurse his fever, the heart-sickness became incurable. Bidden to kill her fondness by dis-

courtesy, he could think of no harsher manner
than riding away without farewell, and there is
nothing left for Elaine but fading and the grave.
And in death she speaks—once, eloquently—
to all :

> And when the heat is gone from out my heart,
> Then take the little bed on which I died
> For Lancelot's love, and deck it like the Queen's
> For richness, and me also like the Queen
> In all I have of rich, and lay me on it.
> And let there be prepared a chariot-bier
> To take me to the river, and a barge
> Be ready on the river, clothed in black.
> I go in state to court, to meet the Queen.
> There surely I shall speak for mine own self,
> And none of you can speak for me so well.
> And therefore let our dumb old man alone
> Go with me, he can steer and row, and he
> Will guide me to that palace, to the doors.
>
> .   .   .   .   .   .
>
> Then came the fine Gawain and wonder'd at her,
> And Lancelot later came and mused at her,
> And last the Queen herself and pitied her.

Her own " little song," her fittest epitaph, is

THE SONG OF LOVE AND DEATH

> Sweet is true love tho' given in vain, in vain ;
> And sweet is death who puts an end to pain :
> I know not which is sweeter, no, not I.
>
> Love, art thou sweet ? then bitter death must be :
> Love, thou art bitter ; sweet is death to me.
> O Love, if death be sweeter, let me die.

> Sweet love, that seems not made to fade away,
> Sweet death, that seems to make us loveless clay,
> I know not which is sweeter, no, not I.
>
> I fain would follow love, if that could be ;
> I needs must follow death, who calls for me ;
> Call and I follow, I follow ! let me die.

It is verily an Idyll of what might have been.
As Arthur felt, her children would have been
noble issue, worthy her fame and name ; but
now

> The shackles of an old love straiten'd him,
> His honour rooted in dishonour stood,
> And faith unfaithful kept him falsely true.

So sin does its work upon the bravest, the most
courteous, the fairest of all.

Tennyson, as we have seen, long hesitated in
approaching "The Holy Grail " : partly from
reverence toward so sacred a subject, but partly
also because it revealed the spiritual centre of
the whole " Idylls," and must therefore be as near
perfection as is humanly possible.   After years
of meditating it came with a " breath of inspiration."

Its real significance lies in Arthur's attitude
toward the Quest.   He not only stands aside
but even protests against it, because

> The King must guard
> That which he rules, and is but as the hind
> To whom a space of land is given to plow,
> *Who may not wander from the allotted field*
> *Before his work is done.*

TENNYSON & HIS POETRY

For him and his knights God wills the active
life : not that of one

> Who, leaving human wrongs to right themselves
> Cares but to pass into the silent life.

And since they are

But men

> With strength and will to right the wrong'd, power
> To lay the sudden heads of violence flat.

Only for one whose work is finished

> Let visions of the night or of the day
> Come, as they will ; and many a time they come,
> Until this earth he walks on seems not earth,
> This light that strikes his eyeballs is not light,
> This air that smites his forehead is not air
> But vision—yea, his very hand and foot—
> *In moments when he feels he cannot die,*
> *And knows himself no vision to himself,*
> *Nor the high God a vision,* nor that One
> Who rose again.

As Tennyson said himself, the passages itali-
cized are " the (spiritually) central lines of the
Idylls." They express his " strong feeling as
to the Reality of the Unseen." Arthur's summary of his work and his visions is " intended
to be the summing up of all in the highest note
by the highest of men." It was inspired by one
of those moments in which the poet " felt and
knew the flesh to be the vision, God and the
spiritual the only real and true."

It is noteworthy, in this most imaginative of

97

TENNYSON & HIS POETRY

all his poems, how variously the Grail appears
to different men ; though it is accompanied
for all by strange sounds and upheavals of
nature.   The holy Nun, of " all but utter white-
ness," tells Sir Percivale :

> Sweet brother, I have seen the Holy Grail :
> For, waked at dead of night, I heard a sound
> As of a silver horn from o'er the hills
> Blown, and I thought, " It is not Arthur's use
> To hunt by moonlight ; " and the slender sound
> As from a distance beyond distance grew
> Coming upon me—O never harp nor horn,
> Nor aught we blow with breath, or touch with hand,
> Was like that music as it came ; and then
> Stream'd thro' my cell a cold and silver beam,
> And down the long beam stole the Holy Grail,
> Rose-red with beatings in it, as if alive,
> Till all the white walls of my cell were dyed
> With rosy colours leaping on the wall ;
> And then the music faded, and the Grail
> Pass'd, and the beam decay'd, and from the walls
> The rosy quiverings died into the night.

Even in her telling of it he saw her eyes

> Beyond my knowing of them, beautiful,
> Beyond all knowing of them, wonderful,
> Beautiful in the light of holiness.

She it was who sent for Sir Galahad, " the
youngest ever made a knight,"

> Saying, " My knight, my love, my knight of heaven,
> O thou, my love, whose love is one with mine,
> I, maiden, round thee, maiden, bind my belt.

Go forth, for thou shalt see what I have seen,
And break thro' all, till one will crown thee king
Far in the spiritual city : '' and as she spake
She sent the deathless passion in her eyes
Thro' him, and made him hers, and laid her mind
On him, and he believed in her belief.

And Galahad saw the Grail :

I saw the fiery face as of a child
That smote itself into the bread, and went ;
And hither am I come ; and never yet
Hath what thy sister taught me first to see,
This Holy Thing, fail'd from my side, nor come
Cover'd, but moving with me night and day,
Fainter by day, but always in the night
Blood-red, and sliding down the blacken'd marsh
Blood-red, and on the naked mountain top
Blood-red, and in the sleeping mere below
Blood-red.

To simple Sir Bors again—" if ever loyal man and true could see it, thou hast seen the Grail " —came a simple vision, befitting the blunt soldier, of which he might not speak :

Beyond all hopes of mine,
Who scarce had pray'd or ask'd it for myself—
Across the seven clear stars—O grace to me—
In colour like the fingers of a hand
Before a burning taper, the sweet Grail
Glided and past.

To these three was granted, however, a full and complete vision. Lancelot and Percivale

saw and saw not. The former, gript by the
sense of sin, and after many journeyings in
frenzied haste, as in a dream, climbed " a
thousand steps with pain " up to a door, and
in his madness he " essay'd the door."

> And thro' a stormy glare, a heat
> As from a seventimes-heated furnace, I,
> Blasted and burnt, and blinded as I was,
> With such a fierceness that I swoon'd away—
> O, yet methought I saw the Holy Grail,
> All pall'd in crimson samite, and around
> Great angels, awful shapes, and wings and eyes.
> And but for all my madness and my sin,
> And then my swooning, I had sworn I saw
> That which I saw ; but what I saw was veil'd
> And cover'd ; and this Quest was not for me.

Percivale's own story occupies most of the
Idyll ; and it is he who tells of the others.   His
Quest reveals much strange symbolism, suggesting the " preparation " needed by common
men for high experiences.

> And I was lifted up in heart, and thought
> Of all my late-shown prowess in the lists,
> How my strong lance had beaten down the knights,
> So many and famous names ; and never yet
> Had heaven appear'd so blue, nor earth so green,
> For all my blood danced in me, and I knew
> That I should light upon the Holy Grail.

> Thereafter, the dark warning of our King,
> That most of us would follow wandering fires,
> Came like a driving gloom across my mind.

Then every evil word I had spoken once,
And every evil thought I had thought of old,
And every evil deed I ever did,
Awoke and cried, "This Quest is not for thee."
And lifting up mine eyes, I found myself
Alone, and in a land of sand and thorns,
And I was thirsty even unto death ;
And I, too, cried, "This Quest is not for thee."

   And on I rode, and when I thought my thirst
Would slay me, saw deep lawns, and then a brook,
With one sharp rapid, where the crisping white
Play'd ever back upon the sloping wave,
And took both ear and eye ; and o'er the brook
Were apple-trees, and apples by the brook
Fallen, and on the lawns. "I will rest here,"
I said, "I am not worthy of the Quest ; "
But even while I drank the brook, and ate
The goodly apples, all these things at once
Fell into dust, and I was left alone,
And thirsting, in a land of sand and thorns.

   And then behold a woman at a door
Spinning ; and fair the house whereby she sat,
And kind the woman's eyes and innocent
And all her bearing gracious ; and she rose
Opening her arms to meet me, as who should say
"Rest here ; " but when I touched her, lo ! she
    too,
Fell into dust and nothing, and the house
Became no better than a broken shed,
And in it a dead babe ; and also this
Fell into dust, and I was left alone.

   And on I rode, and greater was my thirst.
Then flash'd a yellow gleam across the world,

And where it smote the plowshare in the field,
The plowman left his plowing, and fell down
Before it ; where it glitter'd on her pail,
The milkmaid left her milking, and fell down
Before it, and I knew not why, but thought,
" The sun is rising," tho' the sun had risen.
Then was I ware of one that on me moved
In golden armour with a crown of gold
About a casque all jewels ; and his horse
In golden armour jewell'd everywhere :
And on the splendour came, flashing me blind ;
And seem'd to me the Lord of all the world,
Being so huge.   But when I thought he meant
To crush me, moving on me, lo ! he, too,
Opened his arms to embrace me as he came,
And up I went and touch'd him, and he, too,
Fell into dust, and I was left alone
And wearying in a land of sand and thorns.

And I rode on and found a mighty hill,
And on the top, a city wall'd : the spires
Prick'd with incredible pinnacles into heaven.
And by the gateway stirr'd a crowd ; and these
Cried to me climbing, " Welcome, Percivale !
Thou mightiest and thou purest among men ! "
And glad was I and clomb, but found at top
No man, nor any voice.   And thence I past
Far thro' a ruinous city, and I saw
That man had once dwelt there ; but there I found
Only one man of an exceeding age.
" Where is that goodly company," said I,
" That so cried out upon me ? " and he had
Scarce any voice to answer, and yet gasp'd,
" Whence and what art thou ? " and even as he
    spoke

Fell into dust, and disappear'd, and I
Was left alone once more, and cried in grief,
" Lo, if I find the Holy Grail itself
And touch it, it will crumble into dust."

And thence I dropt into a lowly vale,
Low as the hill was high, and where the vale
Was lowest, found a chapel and thereby
A holy hermit in a hermitage,
To whom I told my phantoms, and he said :

" O son, thou hast not true humility,
The highest virtue, mother of them all ;
For when the Lord of all things made Himself
Naked of glory for His mortal change,
' Take thou my robe,' she said, ' for all is thine,'
And all her form shone forth with sudden light
So that the angels were amazed, and she
Follow'd Him down, and like a flying star
Led on the grey-hair'd wisdom of the east ;
But her thou hast not known : for what is this
Thou thoughtest of thy prowess and thy sins ?
Thou hast not lost thyself to save thyself
As Galahad."

Then meeting Galahad, he is drawn to be " one
with him, to believe as he believed." Together
they ride onward, where

Rose a hill that none but man could climb,
Scarr'd with a hundred wintry watercourses—
Storm at the top, and when we gain'd it, storm
Round us and death ; for every moment glanced
His silver arms and gloom'd : so quick and thick
The lightnings here and there to left and right
Struck, till the dry old trunks about us, dead,

Yea, rotten with a hundred years of death,
Sprang into fire : and at the base we found
On either hand, as far as eye could see,
A great black swamp and of an evil smell
Part black, part whiten'd with the bones of men,
Not to be crost, save that some ancient king
Had built a way, where, link'd with many a
    bridge,
A thousand piers ran into the great Sea.
And Galahad fled along them bridge by bridge,
And every bridge as quickly as he crost
Sprang into fire and vanish'd, tho' I yearn'd
To follow ; and thrice above him all the heavens
Open'd and blazed with thunder such as seem'd
Shoutings of all the sons of God : and first
At once I saw him far on the great Sea,
In silver-shining armour starry-clear ;
And o'er his head the holy vessel hung
Clothed in white samite or a luminous cloud.
And with exceeding swiftness ran the boat
If boat it were—I saw not whence it came.
And when the heavens open'd and blazed again
Roaring, I saw him like a silver star—
And had he set the sail, or had the boat
Become a living creature clad with wings ?
And o'er his head the holy vessel hung
Redder than any rose, a joy to me,
For now I knew the veil had been withdrawn.
Then in a moment when they blazed again
Opening, I saw the least of little stars
Down on the waste, and straight beyond the star
I saw the spiritual city and all her spires
And gateways in a glory like one pearl—
No larger, tho' the goal of all the saints—
Strike from the sea ; and from the star there shot

> A rose-red sparkle to the city, and there
> Dwelt, and I knew it was the Holy Grail,
> Which never eyes on earth again shall see.

As Galahad was borne to Heaven, Percivale the Pure " had pass'd into the silent life of prayer." So ends the Quest.

In " Pelleas and Ettarre " the shadows deepen. We read, almost throughout the Idyll, of open sin—the wanton scoffing at the Ideal, more flagrantly than Vivien and more directly attacking Arthur's own company. Pelleas, newly knighted, may with some justice be called " Sir Baby " despite the " young beauty " of his soul :

> For out of the waste islands had he come,
> Where saving his own sisters he had known
> Scarce any but the women of his isles,
> Rough wives, that laugh'd and scream'd against
>   the gulls,
> Makers of nets, and living from the sea.

Inevitably, he is no match for the " great lady " Ettarre, whose

> Mind was bent
> On hearing, after trumpet blown, her name
> And title, Queen of Beauty, in the lists,

whose " violet eyes," round limbs and " dawn-kindled " bloom " abash'd the boy."

Easily feigning a love that could never have deceived an older man, she leads him in triumph to " the Tournament of Youth " (from which Arthur had purposely withheld " his older and

105

his mightier ''), and wins, through him, the
'' sword and golden circlet.'' Then follows dis-
illusion. Riding homeward with his '' lady-
love,'' Pelleas finds the gates closed in his face ;
and by modest persistence (imagining she would
but test his faith) turns her '' scorn to wrath,''
her '' wrath to hate '' ; till at last he understands and leaves her—still with fair words :

> I had liefer ye were worthy of my love,
> Than to be loved again of you—farewell.

There follows the miserable episode of Gawain
offering to '' tame his lady '' for Pelleas, and
traitorously wooing her for himself. The innocent is lashed at last to scorn and fury. Staring
at her towers, he cries :

> O towers so strong,
> Huge, solid, would that even while I gaze
> The crack of earthquake shivering to your base
> Split you, and Hell burst up your harlot roofs
> Bellowing, and charr'd you thro' and thro' within,
> Black as the harlot's heart—hollow as a skull !
> Let the fierce east scream thro' your eyelet-holes,
> And whirl the dust of harlots round and round
> In dung and nettles ! hiss, snake—I saw him
> there—
> Let the fox bark, let the wolf yell. Who yells
> Here in the still sweet summer night, but I—
> I, the poor Pelleas whom she call'd her fool ?
> Fool, beast—he, she, or I ? myself most fool ;
> Beast too, as lacking human wit—disgraced,
> Dishonour'd all for trial of true love—

Love ?—we be all alike : only the King
Hath made us fools and liars. O noble vows !
O great and sane and simple race of brutes
That own no lust because they have no law !
For why should I have loved her to my shame ?
I loathe her, as I loved her to my shame.

Meeting Lancelot :

"I have no name," he shouted, "a scourge
    am I,
To lash the treasons of the Table Round."
"Yea, but thy name ? "   " I have many names,"
    he cried :
" I am wrath and shame and hate and evil fame,
And like a poisonous wind I pass to blast
And blaze the crime of Lancelot and the Queen."

The idealism of the Table cannot live ; Evil sees
triumph at hand.
    " The Last Tournament " carries gloom and
sin yet further.   True, Mark receives punishment, but his murderer has small right to judgment.   Tristram, indeed, has fallen from high
estate : deserting Isolt " patient and prayer-
ful " for Isolt of Britain with her " black-blue
Irish eyes and Irish hair."

Free love—free field—we love but while we may :
The woods are hush'd, their music is no more :
The leaf is dead, the yearning past away :
New leaf, new life—the days of frost are o'er :
New life, new love, to suit the newer day :
New loves are sweet as those that went before :
Free love—free field—we love but while we may.

" The vow that binds too strictly snaps itself," and so, at this last sad " Tournament of the Dead Innocence," the ladies, missing the courtesy of past days, doff the white robes ordered for this joust by Arthur and now " somewhat draggled at the skirt." Arthur's court hath no more its proud answer to the message of the Red Knight :

> Tell thou the King and all his liars, that I
> Have founded my Round Table in the North,
> And whatsoever his own knights have sworn
> My knights have sworn the counter to it—and
>   say
> My tower is full of harlots, like his court,
> But mine are worthier, seeing they profess
> To be none other than themselves—and say
> My knights are all adulterers like his own,
> But mine are truer, seeing they profess
> To be none other ; and say his hour is come,
> The heathen are upon him, his long lance
> Broken, and his Excalibur a straw.

The poet, indeed, will not dwell upon the sadder issues, or even narrate the last fight and defeat. He closes rather upon a personal note, the repentance of Guinevere, following public conviction. Definitely discovered, after years of watching, by the jealous Modred,

> Stammering and staring : it was their last hour,
> A madness of farewells,

the Queen and Lancelot, accepting an end of all things, at last take " the divided way " : he

"back to his land," she to the convent of
Almesbury. Even here shame pursues her in
the form of a little prattling novice, who in all
innocence, not knowing the Queen, will be ever
talking of the wicked Guinevere—"for me, I
thank the Saints I am not great."

Then Arthur, fresh from fight with Lancelot,
with whom he had thought to find her, comes
with his somewhat lofty forgiveness — "as
Eternal God forgives." It is his "doom" that
he loves her still—"let no man dream but
that I love thee still."

> Yet must I leave thee, woman, to thy shame.
> I hold that man the worst of public foes
> Who either for his own or children's sake,
> To save his blood from scandal, lets the wife
> Whom he knows false, abide and rule the house :
> For being thro' his cowardice allow'd
> Her station, taken everywhere for pure,
> She like a new disease, unknown to men,
> Creeps, no precaution used, among the crowd,
> Makes wicked lightning of her eyes, and saps
> The fealty of our friends, and stirs the pulse
> With devil's leaps, and poisons half the young.
> Worst of the worst were that man he that
>   reigns !
> Better the King's waste hearth and aching heart
> Than thou reseated in thy place of light,
> The mockery of my people, and their bane.

The doctrine, one feels, has a touch of that
hardness which seems inseparable from idealism;
and would offer small consolation to average

humanity, in the somewhat high-flown hope for
an after meeting " before high God," when she
may " spring to him and claim him thine."
Guinevere already had " thought she could
not breathe in that fine air, that pure severity
of perfect light," but, to the poet's fancy,
now holds him " the highest and most human
too " :

> Ah my God,
> What might I not have made of Thy fair
> world,
> Had I but loved Thy highest creature here ?
> It was my duty to have loved the highest :
> It surely was my profit had I known :
> It would have been my pleasure had I seen.
> We need must love the highest when we see it,
> Not Lancelot, nor another.

Thus, grown spiritual through forgiveness, the
once proud Queen passes her life in the convent,
for three years its " chosen abbess."

Tennyson, as we know, did not finally complete his Arthurian cycle with Guinevere ; since
the " Morte d'Arthur," rechristened " The
Passing of Arthur," and, with considerable
revisions, must form the real close of the whole
tale. It tells of the mystic " Battle of the
West," fought under a " death-white mist,"
wherein " the king who fights his people fights
himself " ; of weakly affectionate denyings of
Bedivere, " first made and latest left of all the
knights " and his last vision of Excalibur ; of
the slaying of Modred and Arthur's last rest in the
"dusky barge." Over all hangs that fanciful

and " symbolic " atmosphere introduced by the birth of Arthur and hovering about his saintliness throughout the poem.

One need not balance too precisely between our admiration of the spiritual music in the description of the " hand " that carried away his sword, or the Queens who bore off the King. First :

> The great brand
> Made lightnings in the splendour of the moon,
> And flashing round and round, and whirl'd in an arch,
> Shot like a streamer of the northern morn,
> Seen where the moving isles of winter shock
> By night, with noises of the Northern Sea.
> So flash'd and fell the brand Excalibur :
> But ere he dipt the surface, rose an arm
> Clothed in white samite, mystic, wonderful,
> And caught him by the hilt, and brandish'd him
> Three times, and drew him under in the mere.

And again :

> Then saw they how there hove a dusky barge,
> Dark as a funeral scarf from stem to stern,
> Beneath them ; and descending they were ware
> That all the decks were dense with stately forms
> Black-stoled, black-hooded, like a dream—by these
> Three Queens with crowns of gold—and from them rose
> A cry that shiver'd to the tingling stars,
> And, as it were one voice, an agony
> Of lamentation, like a wind, that shrills
> All night in a waste land, where no one comes,
> Or hath come, since the making of the world.

113

To Bedivere, alone, it seems indeed

> The true old times are dead
> When every morning brought a noble chance,
> And every chance brought out a noble knight.

But Arthur " answer'd slowly from the barge " :

> The old order changeth, giving place to new,
> And God fulfils himself in many ways,
> Lest one good custom should corrupt the world.

X

IN the pause between the two groups of " Idylls " (as published) Tennyson issued a volume, itself one of his most popular, containing a poem which may well serve for an introduction to the group, mentioned already but not analyzed, which endeared him perhaps more than any to the hearts of the English people. " Enoch Arden " (1864)—written in about a fortnight—could scarcely have been told with less subtlety ; as the poet himself remarks, even the similes are all such as might have been used by simple fisher-folk. It was followed by many a noble " Idyll of the Hearth," such as, indeed, he had attempted as early as in the 1842 volumes, but which were now destined to be the vehicle of some of his best work.

" Enoch Arden " itself, on a theme suggested by Woolner, is entirely without that humour, racy of the soil, which enlivens " The Northern

Farmer " and others of this group ; but it has all the force of direct narrative fired with sympathy and understanding. There are a thousand details which give the picture a tender reality wedded to a fine imagination that yet never carries us above the subject. "The little wife " and her playmates grow up before us in that quiet " beach a hundred years ago " : and

> Either fixt his heart
> On that one girl ; and Enoch spoke his love,
> But Philip loved in silence.

Then follow the ordinary events of a fishing village, as the sailor and his young bride find a family around them and experience the ups and downs which constitute average daily life. The long voyage, undertaken against her will under stress of poverty ; her rather poor-spirited attempt at shopkeeping ; no news, and the long-delayed acceptance of Philip in place of Enoch—such events have no doubt been happening, and will happen, around us everywhere. The wanderer's return and his unselfish determination to leave wife and children in their prosperous and happy home attain the height of domestic pathos. His sacrifice is no less spontaneous and simple-minded than his wooing had been. Only when dying he charges the garrulous landlady with a last message to his Annie :

> When you shall see her, tell her that I died
> Blessing her, praying for her, loving her ;
> Save for the bar between us, loving her

H   113

As when she laid her head beside my own.
And tell my daughter Annie, whom I saw
So like her mother, that my latest breath
Was spent in blessing her and praying for her.
And tell my son that I died blessing him.
And say to Philip that I blest him too ;
He never meant us anything but good.
But if my children care to see me dead,
Who hardly knew me living, let them come,
I am their father ; but she must not come,
For my dead face would vex her after-life.
And now there is but one of all my blood,
Who will embrace me in the world-to-be :
This hair is his : she cut it off and gave it,
And I have borne it with me all these years,
And thought to bear it with me to my grave ;
But now my mind is changed, for I shall see him,
My babe in bliss : wherefore when I am gone,
Take, give her this, for it may comfort her.

Once only, in his description of the lost
sailor's solitude, does the poet allow himself that
loftiness of language which belongs naturally to
the written word :

The mountain wooded to the peak, the lawns
And winding glades high up like ways to
        Heaven,
The slender coco's drooping crown of plumes,
The lightning flash of insect and of bird,
The lustre of the long convolvuluses
That coil'd around the stately stems, and ran
Ev'n to the limit of the land, the glows
And glories of the broad belt of the world,
All these he saw ; but what he fain had seen

He could not see, the kindly human face,
Nor ever hear a kindly voice, but heard
The myriad shriek of wheeling ocean-fowl,
The league-long roller thundering on the reef,
The moving whisper of huge trees that branch'd
And blossom'd in the zenith, or the sweep
Of some precipitous rivulet to the wave,
As down the shore he ranged, or all day long
Sat often in the seaward-gazing gorge,
A shipwreck'd sailor, waiting for a sail.
No sail from day to day, but every day
The sunrise broken into scarlet shafts
Among the palms and ferns and precipices ;
The blaze upon the waters to the east ;
The blaze upon his island overhead ;
The blaze upon the waters to the west ;
Then the great stars that globed themselves in
        Heaven,
The hollower-bellowing ocean, and again
The scarlet shafts of sunrise—but no sail.

The small volume contains a varied assort-
ment of the kinds of work to which Tennyson's
later years were mainly devoted. " The Grandmother," which quite " upset " Carlyle, was
inspired by Jowett's report of an old lady's saying that " the spirits of her children always
seemed to hover about her " ; and repeats, in
briefer manner with the addition of dialect, the
retrospective atmosphere of domestic melancholy which characterizes " Enoch Arden," as
" Sea Dreams," haunted again by wave melodies, shows equal patience in plain suffering.
" Alymer's Field," a paler " Locksley Hall,"

reveals the old fire—which tyranny had never failed to excite—against

> These old pheasant-lords,
> These partridge-breeders of a thousand years,
> Who had mildew'd in their thousands, doing
>   nothing.

His " little fable," or " universal apologue,"
" The Flower " (so often " narrowed into personality " by its interpreters), illustrates his life-long habits of minute observation, in which friends had noticed him " stop short in a sentence to listen to a blackbird's song, to watch the sunlight glint on a butterfly's wing, or to examine a field-flower at his feet." The flower in this case was a love-in-idleness, and we are told that the verses were " nearly all made on the spot."

THE FLOWER

Once in a golden hour
   I cast to earth a seed.
Up there came a flower,
   The people said, a weed.

To and fro they went
   Thro' my garden bower,
And muttering discontent
   Cursed me and my flower.

Then it grew so tall
   It wore a crown of light,
But thieves from o'er the wall
   Stole the seed by night.

Sow'd it far and wide
　By every town and tower,
Till all the people cried,
　" Splendid is the flower."

Read my little fable :
　He that runs may read.
Most can raise the flowers now,
　For all have got the seed.

And some are pretty enough,
　And some are poor indeed ;
And now again the people
　Call it but a weed.

The spirited " Welcome to Alexandra " affords proof, if proof were needed, of Tennyson's peculiar fitness for the Laureateship. It would be hard to find any " officially inspired " poem in the language so instinct with natural dignity, truly poetical, and no less acceptable to the people at large than to those for whom they were written. In his time, at any rate, one could feel that a poet-laureate could be, what he should always have been, at once a courtier, a patriot, and the voice of a nation. Here again his innate chivalry and true gentlehood provided the noblest stimulus to the honour of literature and country.

THE WELCOME TO ALEXANDRA
MARCH 7, 1863

Sea-Kings' daughter from over the sea,
　　　　　　Alexandra !
Saxon and Norman and Dane are we,
But all of us Danes in our welcome of thee,
　　　　　　Alexandra !

Welcome her, thunders of fort and of fleet !
Welcome her, thundering cheer of the street !
Welcome her, all things youthful and sweet,
Scatter the blossom under her feet !
Break, happy land, into earlier flowers !
Make music, O bird, in the new-budded bowers !
Blazon your mottoes of blessing and prayer !
Welcome her, welcome her, all that is ours !
Warble, O bugle, and trumpet, blare !
Flags, flutter out upon turrets and towers !
Flames, on the windy headland flare !
Utter your jubilee, steeple and spire !
Clash, ye bells, in the merry March air !
Flash, ye cities, in rivers of fire !
Rush to the roof, sudden rocket, and higher
Melt into stars for the land's desire !
Roll and rejoice, jubilant voice,
Roll as a ground-swell dash'd on the strand,
Roar as the sea when he welcomes the land,
And welcome her, welcome the land's desire,
The sea-kings' daughter as happy as fair,
Blissful bride of a blissful heir,
Bride of the heir of the kings of the sea—
O joy to the people and joy to the throne,
Come to us, love us and make us your own :
For Saxon or Dane or Norman we,
Teuton or Celt, or whatever we be,
We are each all Dane in our welcome of thee,
                                        Alexandra !

And finally we have the immortal " Northern
Farmer "—" old style " ; which must obviously
be read with the " new style " of " The Holy
Grail " volume, published five years later.
Tennyson would not have either of these called
118

" photographs " ; and tells us that each was founded on a single sentence, from which he " conjectured the man." Of the old prototype it is reported that on his death-bed, aged about eighty, he cried out, " God A'mighty little knows what He's about, a-taking me. An' Squire will be so mad an' all." The " new style " was suggested by a rich farmer who used to say, " When I canters my 'erse along the ramper (highway) I 'ears proputty, proputty, proputty." Tennyson always delighted in racy anecdotes of rusticity, of which he was a most dramatic raconteur ; and testimony is undivided as to the accuracy of his reproduction. His fine ear enabled him to use the virile figures of speech known to rustics with startling effect ; and he seldom committed the extravagance of making his dialect unintelligible to cultured readers. Moreover, in adopting their phraseology he penetrated even further than elsewhere into the hearts of plain folk : aided perhaps more than anything else by his vivid appreciation of the best English humour. It is a remarkable fact that our noblest exponent of knighthood and the perfect gentleman should have achieved no less substantial popularity as " the Poet of the People " :

Plowmen, shepherds have I found, and more than once, and still could find,
Sons of God and kings of men in utter nobleness of mind.

The " peasant " of Tennyson, maybe, is

somewhat idealized, as he is certainly mid-Victorian : but he is after all a man and a simple man, with whose nature we have much in common, who has helped to make England what she is. The generations of the future may trust his insight into the manners and thoughts of his own day.

NORTHERN FARMER
OLD STYLE

I

Wheer 'asta beän saw long and meä liggin' 'ere aloän
Noorse ? thoort nowt o' a noorse : whoy, Doctor's
    abeän an' agoän :
Says that I moänt 'a naw moor yaäle : but I beänt a
    fool :
Git ma my yaäle, for I beänt a-gooin' to breäk my
    rule.

II

Doctors, they knaws nowt, for a says what's nawways
    true :
Naw soort o' koind o' use to saäy the things that a do.
I've 'ed my point o' yaäle ivry noight sin' I beän 'ere,
An' I've 'ed my quart ivry market-noight for foorty
    year.

III

Parson's a beän loikewoise, an' a sittin' 'ere o' my
    bed.
" The amoighty's a taäkin o' you to 'issén, my friend,"
    a said,
An' a towd ma my sins, an's toithe were due, an' I
    gied it in hond ;
I done my duty by un, as I 'a done by the lond.

IV

Larn'd a ma' beä. I reckons I 'annot sa mooch to
   larn.
But a cost oop, thot a did, 'boot Bessy Marris's barn.
Thof a knaws I hallus voäted wi' Squoire an choorch
   an' staäte,
An' i' the woost o' toimes I wur niver agin the raäte.

V

An' I hallus comed to 's choorch afoor moy Sally wur
   deäd,
An' 'eerd un a bummin' awaäy loike a buzzard-clock [1]
   ower my yeäd,
An' I niver knaw'd whot a meän'd but I thowt a 'ad
   summut to saäy,
An' I thowt a said whot a owt to 'a said an' I comed
   awaäy.

VII

But Parson a comes an' a goos, an' a says it eäsy an'
   freeä,
" The amoighty's a taäkin o' you to 'issén, my friend,"
   says 'eä.
I weänt saäy men be loiars, thof summun said it in
   'aäste :
But a reäds wonn sarmin a weeäk, an' I' a stubb'd
   Thornaby waäste.

XII

Do godamoighty knaw what a's doing a-taäkin' o'
   meä ?
I beänt wonn as saws 'ere a beän an' yonder a peä ;
An' Squoire 'ull be sa mad an' all—a' dear a' dear !
And I 'a monaged for Squoire come Michaelmas thirty
   year.

[1] Cockchafer.

XIII

A mowt 'a taäken Joänes, as 'ant a 'aäpoth o' sense,
Or a mowt 'a taäken Robins—a niver mended a fence :
But godamoighty a moost taäke meä an' taäke ma now
Wi 'auf the cows to cauve an' Thornaby holms to
    plow !

XIV

Looäk 'ow quoloty smoiles when they sees ma a
    passin' by,
Says to thessén naw doot, " what a mon a beä
    sewer-ly ! "
For they knaws what I beän to Squoire sin fust a
    comed to the 'All ;
I done my duty by Squoire an' I done my duty by all.

XV

Squoire's in Lunnon, an' summun I reckons 'ull 'a to
    wroite,
For who's to howd the lond arter meä thot muddles
    ma quoit ;
Sartin-sewer I beä, thot a weänt niver give it to
    Joänes,
Noither a moänt to Robins—a niver rembles the
    stoäns.

XVI

But summun 'ull come ater meä mayhap wi' 'is kittle
    o' steäm
Huzzin' an' maäzin' the blessed feälds wi' the Divil's
    oän teäm.
Gin I mun doy I mun doy, an' loife they says is
    sweet,
But gin I mun doy I mun doy, for I couldn abear to
    see it.

XVII

What atta stannin' theer for, an' doesn bring ma the
    yaäle ?
Doctor's a 'tottler, lass, an a's hallus i' the owd taäle ;
I weänt breäk rules for Doctor, a knaws naw moor
    nor a floy ;
Git ma my yaäle I tell tha, an' gin I mun doy I mun
    doy.

NORTHERN FARMER

NEW STYLE

I

Dosn't thou 'ear my 'erse's legs, as they canters awaäy ?
Proputty, proputty, proputty—that's what I 'ears 'em
    saäy.
Proputty, proputty, proputty—Sam, thou's an ass for
    thy paäins :
Theer's moor sense i' one o' is legs nor in all thy
    braäins.

II

Woä—theer's a craw to pluck wi' tha, Sam : yon's
    parson's 'ouse—
Dosn't thou knaw that a man mun be eäther a man or
    a mouse ?
Time to think on it then ; for thou'll be twenty to
    weeäk.[1]
Proputty, proputty—woä then woä—let ma 'ear
    mysén speäk.

III

Me an' thy muther, Sammy, 'as beän a-talkin' o' thee ;
Thou's been talkin' to muther, an' she beän a tellin'
    it me.

[1] This week.

Thou'll not marry for munny—thou's sweet upo'
    parson's lass—
Noä—thou'll marry fur luvv—an' we boäth on us
    thinks tha an ass.

IV

Seeä'd her todaäy goä by—Saäint's-daäy—they was
    ringing the bells.
She's a beauty thou thinks—an' soä is scoors o' gells,
Them as 'as munny an' all—wot's a beauty?—the
    flower as blaws.
But proputty, proputty sticks, an' proputty, proputty
    graws.

V

Do'ant be stunt[1]: taäke time: I knaws what maäkes
    tha sa mad.
Warn't I craäzed fur the lasses mysén when I wur a
    lad?
But I knaw'd a Quaäker feller as often 'as towd ma
    this:
"Doänt thou marry for munny, but goä wheer
    munny is!"

VI

An' I went wheer munny war: an' thy mother coom
    to 'and,
Wi' lots o' munny laaid by, an' a nicetish bit o' land.
Maäybe she warn't a beauty:—I niver giv it a thowt—
But warn't she as good to cuddle an' kiss as a lass as
    'ant nowt?

IX

Luvv? what's luvv? thou can luvv thy lass an' 'er
    munny too,
Maakin' 'em goä togither as they've good right to do.

[1] Obstinate.

Could'n I luvv thy muther by cause o' 'er munny
  laaïd by !
Naäy—fur I luvv'd her a vast sight moor fur it :
  reäson why.

XII

Tis'n them as 'as munny as breäks into 'ouses an'
  steäls,
Them as 'as coäts to their backs an' taäkes their
  regular meäls.
Noä, but's its them as niver knaws wheer a meäl's to
  be 'ad.
Taäke my word for it, Sammy, the poor in a loomp
  is bad.

XIII

Them or thir feythers, tha sees, mun' 'a beän a laäzy
  lot,
Fur work mun 'a gone to the gittin' whiniver munny
  was got.
Feyther 'ad ammost nowt ; leästways 'is munny was
  'id.
But 'e tued an' moil'd 'issén deäd, an 'e died a good
  un, 'e did.

XIV

Loook thou theer wheer Wrigglesby beck comes out
  by the 'ill !
Feyther run up to the farm, an' I runs up to the mill ;
An' I'll run up to the brig, an' that thou'll live to see ;
And if thou marries a good un I'll leäve the land to
  thee.

XV

Thim's my noätions, Sammy, wheerby I means to
  stick ;
But if thou marries a bad un, I'll leäve the land to
  Dick.—

TENNYSON & HIS POETRY

Coom oop, proputty, proputty—that's what I 'ears 'im
    saäy—
Proputty, proputty, proputty—canter an' canter
    awaäy.

X

IF the character of Arthur rested mainly
on legend and tradition, Tennyson's
kindred venture, the dramatic trilogy,
was certainly inspired by the study of pure
history. Boldly taking up the work where
Shakespeare left it, he attempts once more to
portray the " making of England."

In " Harold " (1876) Dane, Saxon and Norman are still struggling for supremacy ; people
and clergy together are stirred from lethargy.
" Becket " (1879)[1] deals with a critical period
in that " long-tugged-at, threadbare-worn Quar-
rell of Crown and Church." " Queen Mary "
(1875), showing the downfall of Romanism,
heralds an era of individual freedom. Outside
strict sequence and in lighter vein came " The
Foresters " (1892), a tale of Robin Hood and
Marian, in which he " sketched the state of the
people in another great transition period in the
making of England, when the barons sided
with the people and eventually won for them
the Magna Charta."

Tennyson calls " Harold " a " Tragedy of
Doom." Comet and shipwreck unite against
the noble patriot, whose own acts, without
debasing his character, remain his chief enemies.

[1] Though printed in this year, it was not published till 1884.

126

As Professor Jebb noted in the " Times," his
" false oath by the saints of Normandy gave the
play tragic unity " :

It becomes his avenging destiny. In his short
career it is what the inherited curse was to the house
of Pelope. Harold can say in the true sense which
Euripides meant, " My tongue has sworn, but my soul
has not sworn." Nothing in the play seems to us finer
than the contrast between Harold's own view of his
predicament and the casuistry of the theologians who
seek to reassure him. He has a foreboding that he
must suffer the immediate doom of the defiled ; but
beyond that doom he looks up to that Justice which
shall give him the reward of the pure in spirit.

Aubrey de Vere also wrote that " the great
characteristic of this drama is that of an heroic
strength blended with heroic simplicity, and
everything in it harmonises with that pre-
dominant characteristic." It is Harold's simplicity which gives " quite an extraordinary
pathos to the malicious might of those circumstances which force his feet off the straight way
and into those perplexed paths for which they
have no inclination."

The contrast between his baffled uprightness
and the Norman craft of William, afterwards
Conqueror, shows a command of dialogue
Tennyson seldom equalled.

Tennyson, indeed, seldom mastered the techni-
calities of stage-craft ; and though he allowed
actors to " edit " his plays for the stage (being
" ready," says Mary Anderson, " to sacrifice
even his most beautiful lines for the sake of a

real dramatic effect ''), he did not believe in sensational curtains or approve the omission of character-revealing soliloquies.

In "Harold," undoubtedly, the most powerful passages occur in Act V with its grand battle-scene—a tragic ending to a noble life, and yet, as we read history to-day, the nation's fall was but "the prelude of a new birth"; foreseen, with poetic licence, by the dying Edward.

> Then a great Angel past along the highest
> Crying "the doom of England," and at once
> He stood beside me, in his grasp a sword
> Of lightnings, wherewithal he cleft the tree
> From off the bearing trunk, and hurl'd it from him
> Three fields away, and then he dash'd and drench'd,
> He dyed, he soak'd the trunk with human blood,
> And brought the sunder'd tree again, and set it
> Straight on the trunk, that thus baptized in blood
> Grew ever high and higher, beyond my seeing,
> And shot out sidelong boughs across the deep
> That dropt themselves, and rooted in far isles
> Beyond my seeing : and the great Angel rose
> And past again along the highest crying
> "The doom of England ! "

But it was "Queen Mary," the first written of the historical plays, which was its author's favourite, and probably his most successful. Irving's Philip was admitted a rare triumph; Gladstone welcomed it as a "stroke for the nation"; and Froude declared that he had "hit a more fatal blow than a thousand pamphleteers and controversialists," besides

claiming " one more section of English history
from the wilderness." Tennyson was moved
principally by pity for the woman who, first
degraded by her father and friends, was in the
end abandoned by her husband and hated by her
people. To this tragedy of a bright nature thus
cruelly clouded and to the happier Elizabeth he
devoted his chief energy ; though his portrait
of Cranmer (whose " holy calm " alone pro-
vides adequate artistic relief to the intense
sadness of the whole drama) is masterly ; while
Philip, Courtenay, Lord Howard, Gardiner and
Bonner, Lord Paget, Sir Thomas Wyatt, Sir
Ralph Bagenhall, Sir Thomas White, and even
the imaginary servants and peasants are " all
drawn with a firm hand and painted with a
delicate touch." A few lines of description
bring before us, with true fire, the dogmatic
bishop :

> His big baldness,
> That irritable forelock which he rubs,
> His buzzard beak, and deep incaverned eyes.

The note of tragedy rises with the curtain as
we find the crowd of citizens " cackling of
bastardy under the Queen's own nose," and
already proclaiming the Lady Elizabeth " more
noble and royal." From the beginning 'tis said
openly, " there will be no peace for Mary till
Elizabeth lose her head," and the ambitious
plotting and wooing of Courtenay occupy much
of the first act, while Mary fondles the " most
goodly " miniature of Philip, passionately

crying out against the wrongs of her " sweet mother " and dreaming over her own miseries :

> God has sent me here
> To take such order with all heretics
> That it shall be, before I die, as tho'
> My father and my brother had not lived.

And so it is to the end. Her marriage, more unpopular than the most virulent persecution, brought no personal satisfaction, since Philip was moved by policy from the beginning : neither people nor parliament had any desire for war with France—to please Spain : and the country remained Protestant at heart.

To the commoners it seemed she went on " a-burnin' and a-burnin' to get her baaby born," and for

> The unity of Universal Church,
> Mary would have it ; and this Gardiner follows ;
> The unity of Universal Hell,
> Philip would have it ; and this Gardiner follows !
> A Parliament of imitative apes !
> Sheep at the gap which Gardiner takes, who not
> Believes the Pope, nor any of them believe—
> These spaniel-Spaniard English of the time,
> Who rub their fawning noses in the dust,
> For that is Philip's gold-dust, and adore
> This Vicar of their Vicar.

It may be doubted, moreover, whether *any* statesman was, at *any time*, ruled by personal loyalty to the Queen : and stimulus to treachery was everywhere at hand. The poet has made us

TENNYSON & HIS POETRY

feel that, like Mary herself, we can trust nobody :
and when at last she comes to realize that Philip
had *never* loved her, one can only echo her wish
that Elizabeth may "wear her crown and dance
upon her grave."

To heighten the proper centre of personal
emotion Tennyson allows Mary's passion for
Philip to dominate every turn of events, even in
her absence ; beginning with her fond dwelling
on his portrait and culminating in the eloquent
eulogy of Act III, sc. ii.

> Oh, Philip, husband ! now thy love to mine
> Will cling more close, and those bleak manners
>   thaw,
> That make me shamed and tongue-tied in my
>   love.
> The second Prince of Peace—
> The great unborn defender of the Faith,
> Who will avenge me of mine enemies—
> He comes, and my star rises.
> The stormy Wyatts and Northumberlands,
> The proud ambitions of Elizabeth,
> And all her fieriest partisans—are pale
> Before my star !
> The light of this new learning wanes and dies :
> The ghosts of Luther and Zuinglius fade
> Into the deathless hell which is their doom
> Before my star !
> His sceptre shall go forth from Ind to Ind !
> His sword shall hew the heretic peoples down !
> His faith shall clothe the world that will be his,
> Like universal air and sunshine !   Open,
> Ye everlasting gates !   The King is here !

Yet all the time "many voices call him" away :

> The voices of Castile and Aragon,
> Granada, Naples, Sicily, and Milan,—
> The voices of Franche-Comté, and the Netherlands,
> The voices of Peru and Mexico,
> Tunis, and Oran, and the Philippines,
> And all the fair spice-islands of the East.

His real object in coming to share an English throne had proved unattainable, and he grows weary of even that slight pretence of affection which he had scarcely ever maintained. Verily hers is no case for a "good physician" :

> Drugs—but he knows they cannot help me—says
> That rest is all—tells me I must not think.
> That I must rest—I shall rest by and by.
> Catch the wild cat, cage him, and when he
>   springs
> And maims himself against the bars, say "rest."
> Why, you must kill him if you would have him
>   rest—
> Dead or alive you cannot make him happy.

"Becket" is no less a drama of personal emotion—the tragedy of severed friendship. Tennyson is concerned almost entirely with the passionate relations of Henry and Becket—both "men too headstrong for their office"—and hardly touches the national issue. We see only that here, at least as personified by its Archbishop, the Church does with genuine charity espouse the cause of the people, while the barons are still allied with the King in one tyrannous aristocracy. The play also supports a contention, recently much in favour with certain churchmen, that England never in pre-Protestant days wholly acknowledged the supremacy of Rome. Her leaders put conscience above the Pope, her spiritual dignity above the policy of the Vatican. " Had I been Holy Father," cries Becket,

> I would have done my most to keep Rome holy,
> I would have made Rome know she still is Rome—
> Who stands aghast at her eternal self
> And shakes at mortal kings—her vacillation,
> Avarice, craft—O God, how many an innocent
> Has left his bones upon the way to Rome
> Unwept, uncared for. Yea—on my own self
> The King had had no power except for Rome.
> 'Tis not the King who is guilty of my exile,
> But Rome, Rome, Rome !

Henry describes the early Becket as

> A doter on white pheasant-flesh at feasts,
> A sauce-deviser for thy days of fish,
> A dish-designer, and most amorous
> Of good old red sound liberal Gascon wine.

And Eleanor, his bitterest enemy, approved his helping Henry to break down the barons' castles—" a great and sound policy that : I could embrace him for it : you could not see the King for the kinglings." But, once made archbishop, and, as he feels, representative of God, his impulsive fanaticism dissolves the worldly bond. He is now " over the King " he formerly served with so much zeal. Life becomes a contest for supremacy, in which the primate honestly claims inspiration for deeds and words the most arbitrary. Always, as Henry himself recognizes, "He hates my will, not me." On both sides the controversy centres in matters that seem transient, if not trivial, and really resolves itself into petty and almost formal arguments for the last word. They seem scarcely to disagree about any fundamental, but one is no less obstinate than the other in claiming the right to say "I will" and "thou shalt." Tennyson makes Henry rather more wilful, inasmuch as he has no ideal to excuse his obstinacy, beyond "custom"; whereas Becket is thoroughly sincere in his assumption of spiritual warrant.

There is a mystic element in the sacerdotal which adds dignity to the character; since God in a vision had pronounced, "Thou art the man!" So called, he will labour, without thought of consequences to himself or others, or of loyalty in past brotherhood to his sovereign, day and night unceasingly in the service of God and the honour of Canterbury, for which he will cast aside the warrior's puissance, the Chancellor's wisdom and "all the heap'd experience of life." He is honestly unconscious of his own tendency to "mix his spites and private hates with his defence of heaven": and "like a fool, he knows no middle way." As may be expected, his own followers are not prepared to go to such lengths with him; and an attitude which would be dangerous at any time, becomes suicidal with such a man as the King.

He, with equal arrogance, cries, " Look you, you shall have none other God but me ! " claiming obedience by right of that true kingship, by which he has

> Made the twilight day
> And struck a shape from out the vague, and law
> From madness.

Into this clash and turmoil of will is woven the tender story of Rosamond, an early favourite of Tennyson's, which gave Ellen Terry her opportunity, beside the fine Becket of Irving, whose episodical stage-version was said by him to be " one of the three most successful plays produced at the Lyceum."

As already stated, Tennyson has treated history more lightly in " The Foresters " (1892), though here too we find a shadow of that great struggle which was so soon to secure a real advance in the " making of England." Robin Hood's merrymaking has always a stern purpose—to thwart tyranny. His manner of life suits the times, when the " scatter-brained " Richard, " sacking and wasting towns with random pillage," has " outlaw'd himself and helps nor rich, nor poor," that he may risk his life for " a straw," leaving England to

> One that holds no love is pure
> No friendship sacred, values neither man
> Nor woman save as tools—God help the mark—
> To his unprincely ends.

135

The poet's achievement, however, rests on the fine chivalry of the Maid Marian, of whom Ada Rehan declared that to play her "made her feel for the time a happier and better woman." "There is no land like England," and other songs, are perfect examples of Tennyson's lyrical power ; and the whole picture of forest-life has real gaiety.

His remaining dramas may be (in defiance of chronology) most conveniently dismissed here in a few words. "The Falcon" (1879), indeed, is "an exquisite little poem in action" ; but one cannot accept Irving's tribute to "The Cup" (1880) as a "grand tragedy." The ordinary plot and theorizings of "The Promise of May" (1882) leave us cold, though its songs and dialect scenes recall some of his best work.

XII

THOUGH Tennyson produced no long poem after the Historical Plays, it would be quite untrue to say that his powers showed any symptoms of decline. Later volumes, "The Ballads" of 1880, "Tiresias," "Demeter," and "The Death of Œnone," all gave us poems which none would readily spare, and in which his most marked gifts are conspicuous. His quiet life and regular habits promoted longevity without decay : his mental concentration and singlemindedness produced inevitably continuous advance in execution. Tennyson's interests were comparatively limited, but not having been wasted by extravagance or spiritual wanderings they remained keen to the last.

Though " there is not one touch of biography in them from beginning to end," the two " Locksley Halls " " contain the sum of his politics," the " point of view from which he regarded the world." It is significant that in essentials this remains the same throughout. The earlier poem is emphatically a youthful outburst, but not disordered. It reflects not only his personal outlook on things, but "the tone of the age." The later has equal historical significance, general and personal. It is in some sort a protest against what Lytton called the " silly and pernicious rubbish of Neo-Radicalism," for which his support had been read into " Locksley Hall " ; and he was accordingly accused, with some vehemence, of deserting the ideals of youth. But he was in fact no more conservative or conventional than he had always been. The old lover is exactly what the young lover must have become, only growing " with the growth of age." Though naturally liable to moods of depression, he had " a stronger faith in God and in human goodness." Above all he rests in the hope of Immortality, as the poet himself :

Gone for ever ! Ever ? No—for since our dying
    race began,
Ever, ever, and for ever was the leading light of
    man.

He may lament with heat the "troughs of Zolaism" in which "essayist, atheist, novelist, realist, rhymester" play their parts. He may question with fine scorn whether it be really true that "only those who cannot read can rule." He may rail against those who,

> Yelling with the yelling street,
> Set the feet above the brain and swear the brain
> is in the feet.

He may bid them

> Rip your brothers' vices open, strip your own foul
> passions bare ;
> Down with reticence, down with reverence—for-
> ward—naked—let them stare.

Yet after madness and massacre, schemes and systems, the Earth, "yet young" in the days "I shall not see," shall show us something kindlier, higher, holier, when science has quench'd all diseases and war has died out over a universal harvest.

> All the full-brain, half-brain races, led by Justice,
> love, and truth ;
> All the millions one at length with all the visions
> of my youth.

Though progress was not moving entirely along the lines he had anticipated or desired, Tennyson saw it making toward the same goal. The ideals of his youth remained with him : he

saw the old visions. Therein lay his strength—
the consistent purpose of a lifetime : he always
cared about his fellow-men and about pleasing
them, without bending to what he held transient
and false.

It is, however, "The Ancient Sage," a
" very personal poem," with its " Faith " and
" Passion of the Past," which most intimately
reflects his personal attitude. It is the argument of the city-wearied sage against the
materialism of " one that loved and honour'd
him, and yet was no disciple."

> Thou canst not prove thou art immortal, no
> Nor yet that thou art mortal.

The youth has lost not only faith, but
morality ; yet he is no idle libertine, and it is
a true love he has lost.

> The years that when my youth began
>   Had set the lily and rose
> By all my ways where'er they ran,
>   Have ended mortal foes ;
> My rose of love for ever gone,
>   My lily of truth and trust—
> They made her lily and rose in one,
>   And changed her into dust.
> O rosetree planted in my grief,
>   And growing, on her tomb,
> Her dust is greening in your leaf,
>   Her blood is in your bloom.
> O slender lily waving there,
>   And laughing back the light,
> In vain you tell me " Earth is fair,"
>   When all is dark as night.

To all scepticism the sage has answer, though not proof : " For nothing worthy can be proven, nor yet disproven." There should we

> Cleave ever to the sunnier side of doubt,
> And cling to faith beyond the forms of faith.
>
> .   .   .   .   .   .
>
> Let be thy wail and help thy fellow-men.

It was a personal experience eight-and-twenty years earlier which provided the germ of this instinct for Immortality ; also emphasized in "Vastness" :

> For more than once when I
> Sat all alone, revolving in myself
> The word that is the symbol of myself,
> The mortal limit of the Self was loosed,
> And past into the Nameless, as a cloud
> Melts into Heaven.

Of the four volumes issued between his seventy-second year and his death, at eighty-two,[1] we must now speak in more detail. The "Ballads and Other Poems" (1880) is best remembered by "The Revenge" ; though it also contained "The Defence of Lucknow," "Rizpah," "The First Quarrel," "The Northern Cobbler," and "De Profundis." The title-poem of "Tiresias" (1885) is an important expression of philosophy accompanying "The Ancient Sage." The "Spinster's Sweet-Arts" and "To-morrow" give us his dialect at his best. This volume also contained some fine

[1] To which period, as we have seen, also belong "The Cup," "The Promise of May," and "The Foresters."

Laureate poems ; as did " Demeter " (1889)
with its far-famed " Crossing the Bar "—the
poet's epilogue. Here too came " Merlin and
the Gleam," " The Oak," " Owd Roä,"
" Romney's Romance," and the beautiful
" Far, far Away." Finally " The Death
of Œnone " (1892) contains also " Akbar's
Dream," the dialect " Churchwarden and
Curate," and " Riflemen Form " (reprinted from
the " Times " of 1859). It may be mentioned
in this connexion that the last poem he finished
was " The Dreamer " with its buoyant refrain
of " All's well that ends well." It was written
in anticipation of the end, offering many an
echo of old notes and a summary of faith.

In treating these shorter poems it will be more
convenient to group them by subject or manner
than by volume ; and (after noting his last
return to his favourite theme in the beautiful
lyric of " Merlin and the Gleam ") we shall
begin with those few noble outbursts of patriot-
ism (recalling " The Light Brigade " and " The
Ode on the Death of Duke of Wellington ")
which came with such peculiar fitness from the
Laureate's pen.

Obviously " The Revenge " leads here. Every
schoolboy is familiar with its ringing periods.
" The story," says Froude, " struck a deeper
terror, though it was but the action of a single
ship, into the hearts of the Spanish people ; it
dealt a more deadly blow upon their fame and
moral strength than the Armada itself " ; and
Tennyson, as Carlyle told him, " got the grip

of it.'' There is scarcely less fire or music in
'' The Defence of Lucknow '' with its proud
refrain upon '' the banner of England '' ; or
in '' Riflemen Form ''—written before the
Volunteer movement began. Though the
'' Charge of the Heavy Brigade '' will never be
so popular as its precursor (in part because the
episode itself is less dramatic), one is no way
surprised to learn that one of Scarlett's men
should have read it '' with a renewal of that
blood-rising which I recognized on the day when
we wheeled into line, and started to meet the
big foe above us on that hillside, now twenty
years ago.''

It was this poem which brought to a head the
charge of loving war for its own sake, which
had been more than once whispered against
Tennyson, and prompted the '' Epilogue '' :

> And who loves War for War's own sake,
> Is fool or crazed or worse.

It was, of course, heroism and love of country,
not a lust of the fight, which inspired his pen on
such topics.

> And here the Singer for his art
> Not all in vain may plead,
> The song that nerves a nation's heart
> Is in itself a deed !

A somewhat similar influence, a '' passion for
the past,'' clearly influenced the classical and
legendary group, from which we note that most

of these later titles were derived. Tennyson delighted in this kind of work at times, and always revealed thereby real culture, as witnessed in the lines "To Virgil"—"wielder of the stateliest measure ever moulded by the lips of man." But he had no taste for a "mere réchauffé of old legends," and always gave his antique "a frame—something modern about it." "Demeter and Persephone" was written at his son's request, and expresses with dignity and restraint the great parable of motherhood which had been long a favourite with him, as it must be with all lovers of nature. In "The Death of Œnone" he touches the heart of tragedy, that cry of the deserted which hovers behind the unpeopling of Ilium by one man's treachery; and shows us Paris, type of the handsome undoer, forgiven by the shepherd-playmates and rejoined at last on the burning pyre by his beloved of the valley.

It was, no doubt, Tennyson's love of finding new links between past and present, and of discovering the common humanity in all ages—to him a powerful argument for faith—that directed his mind to the Mogul Akbar, inventor of an eclectic religion, "uniting all creeds, castes and peoples," which seems curiously modern. This "Divine Faith" had no dealings with "either heresy or orthodoxy"; maintaining that in every temple people see God, in every language they praise him. It is small wonder that at the court of Akbar "the sages and learned of all creeds" gathered in "perfect

toleration or peace," while " the perverse and
evil-minded were covered with shame."

'Tis a noble resolve, truly, of the old poet's—
" To pray, to do according to the prayer " : a
noble dream—of a " sacred fane " :

> A temple, neither Pagod, Mosque, nor Church,
> But loftier, simpler, always open-door'd
> To every breath from heaven, and Truth and
>   Peace
> And Love and Justice came and dwelt therein.

A noble hymn to the Sun it was he has put into
the mouth of Akbar :

> Shadow-maker, shadow-slayer, arrowing light from
>   clime to clime,
> Hear thy myriad laureates hail thee monarch in
>   their woodland rhyme.
>   Warble bird, and open flower, and, men, below
>   the dome of azure
> Kneel adoring Him the Timeless in the flame that
>   measures Time !

In " De Profundis " Tennyson expresses what
may be called the opposite end of Immortality :
welcoming the child—" the perfect prophet of
the man " :

> From that great deep, before our world begins,
>
> .   .   .   .   .   .
>
> From that true world within the world we see.

In " Tiresias " he links his lifelong friendship
for the ever-candid Fitzgerald to a charming

picture of the vegetarian philosopher, in which, by the way, is disclosed one secret of his great gift of nature-painting, itself proving how nature had long found her way into his very being. Referring to the " vegetarian dream " of this poem Tennyson tells us : " I never saw any landscape that came up to the landscapes I have seen in my dreams. The mountains of Switzerland seem insignificant compared with the mountains I have imagined." It was a mutton chop, following six weeks of vegetables, that brought before his dream-vision " the vines of the south, with huge Eschol branches, trailing over the glaciers of the north."

" Tiresias " embodies much of his whole philosophy, " with all the boundless yearning of the prophet's heart." Here we read that " Virtue must shape itself in deed," that " the golden lyre is ever sounding " in the heroic ears of those who dare

> For that sweet motherland which gave them birth,
> Nobly to do, nobly to die.

The lyric Prologue and Epilogue, twin tributes to friendship, " truly rank among masterpieces of rendering, in pure poetry, the humorous and pathetic sides of common life ; balanced evenly between realistic and ideal treatment."

The fine record of " Romney's Remorse," whose wife's forgiveness was " worth all his pictures, even as a matter of art," links these book-inspired poems to those founded on observation of life around him : among which, again, "Rizpah," or "Bones," stands somewhat apart in its grimly dramatic adaptation of a tale chance showed him in a penny local magazine called "Old Brighton" :

Do you think I care for *my* soul if my boy be gone to the fire ?

"To-morrow" (its Irish corrected from Carleton's "Traits of the Irish Peasantry") is less grim in its tale of the woman whose "wits wor dead" through long waiting for her lost lover. The bog had him, and kept him, while many another wooed fair Molly in vain.

Achora, yer laste little whisper was sweet as the lilt of a bird !
Acushla, ye set my heart batin' to music wi' every word !
An' sorra the Queen wid her sceptre in sich an illigant han',
An' the fall of yer foot in the dance was as light as the snow on the lan',
An' the sun kem out of a cloud whiniver ye walkt in the shtreet.

Truly it seems like "a bit of yestherday in a dhrame."

Of "The Sisters," again, we feel the silent tragedy somewhat softened by its narration as a tale of the past (it had been actually "heard" by Tennyson) ; though here marriage brought indeed but the twilight of its natural joy when

That dead bridesmaid, meant to be my bride,
Put forth cold hands between us.

146

"The Ring," told with great detail, gives a more melodramatic, and on the whole less pleasing, catastrophe to a similar situation : and, for all its hopelessness, does not quite equal the short story which Henry James made from the legend that he and Tennyson both learnt from Lowell. It was Miss Gladstone who told him of Emmie and 'her dear, long, lean little arms,' of "In the Children's Hospital," where nurse so distrusted the new rough doctor muttering, " all very well, but the good Lord Jesus has had His day." The simply pathetic "First Quarrel," with its record of sharp punishment for a hard word—since "By-gones ma'be come again," came from his own Isle of Wight.

Very similar in atmosphere, but nearly always lightened by humour, we have here the poems in dialect, mostly of Lincolnshire, among which one only—"The Village Wife : or The Entail "—was an actual portrait of one who " thowt 'twere the will o' the Lord, but Miss Annie she said it wur drains."

The vigour of description is extraordinary, whether it be the bookish squire who

. . . sit like a graät glimmer-gowk wi' 'is glasses
　　athurt 'is noäse,
An' 'is noäse sa grafted wi' snuff es it couldn't be
　　scroob'd awaäy ;

the son, whose like could not be found,

　　　　　　'E were that outdacious at 'oam
Not thaw ye went fur to raäke out Hell wi' a small-
　　tooth coämb ;

147

or his " darter," who

> . . . rampaged about wi' their grooms, an' was
> 'untin' arter the men,
> An' hallus a-dallackt an' dizen'd out, an' a-buyin'
> new cloäthes.

We all know how Charlie, asked to cut off the
entail and save the " gells " from the Ouse,
swore " Noa. I've gotten the staäte by the
taäil an' be dang'd if I iver let goa ! " Naturally
the obstinate boy " brok' 'is neck " ; squire was
soon buried " smiling," and " nawbody "
would have the girls, of whom one " wur
lame," another " weak in th' hattics, wi'out
any harm i' the legs " : and each had her
special misfortune. "So new squire's coom'd
wi' is taäil."

It was memory of a tale heard in early youth
that a man did actually set up a bottle of gin in
his window " to defy the drink " which inspired
" The Northern Cobbler," with its splendid
flavour of strong language.

> Stan' 'im theer i' the naäme o' the Lord an' the power
> ov 'is Graäce,
> Stan' 'im theer, fur I'll loök my hennemy strait i' the
> faäce.
> .   .   .   .   .   .
> Wouldn't a pint 'a sarved as well as a quart ?   Now
> doubt :
> But I liked a bigger feller to fight wi' an' fowt it out.
> .   .   .   .   .   .
> I'll hev 'im a-buried wi'mma an' taäke 'im afoor the
> Throän.

148

Every line tells ; and how much is compressed
in that one phrase about the parson who calls
him a " Methody man " : " An' Muggins 'e
preäch'd o' Hell-fire an' the loov o' God fur
men." The reverse attitude towards the preaching appears in " The Churchwarden and the
Curate," where the old man exhorts " parson's
lad," just ordained, against speaking his mind
like his father—" *He'll* niver swop Owlby an'
Scralby fur owt but the Kingdon of Heaven."

Tha mun tackle the sins o' the Wo'ld, an' not the
    faults o' the Squire.
An' I reckon tha'll light of a livin' somewheers i' the
    Wowd or the Fen,
If tha cottons down to tha betters, an' keäps thysen to
    thysen.
But niver not speäk plaäin out, if thou wants to git
    forrard a bit,
But creeäp along the hedge-bottoms, an' thar'll be a
    Bishop yet.

His philosophy, moreover, does not forbid the
indulgence of private spite, as the curate is given
permission to " speak hout to the Baptises,"

Fur they leäved their nasty sins i' *my* pond, an' it
    poison'd the cow.

No wonder the good man is a friend to
" Quoloty " and " gits the plaäte fuller o'
Soondays nor ony chuchwarden afoor."
    The almost hidden pathos of " The Spinster's
Sweet-Arts " has a delicate humour of its own
subtly varied from these ; and the old lady

knows well enough, recalling " the fellers "—
" it warn't not me es wur pretty, but my two
'oondered a-year." Her gentle sarcasms on the
men have no bitterness ; only she fancies her
own way and has " naw likin' fur brats."

An' I sit in my oän little parlour, an' sarved by my
    oän little lass,
Wi' my oän little garden outside, an' my oän bed o'
    sparrow-grass,
An' my oän door-poorch wi' the woodbine an' jessmine
    a' dressin' it greeän,
An' my oän fine Jackman i' purple a' roäbin' the 'ouse
    like a Queeän.

Her experience of "sweet-arts" was pleasant
enough, but " a man be a durty thing, a trouble
an' plague wi'indoor."

So I likes 'em best wi' taäils when they 'even't a
    woord to saäy.

If the spinster owed a quiet happiness to her
cats, certainly the farmer " owd Roäver moor
nor he iver owäd mottal man " :

Fur 'e's moor good sense na the Parliament man 'at
    stans fur us 'ere,
An' I'd vote fur 'im, my oän sen, if 'e could but stan
    fur the shire.

" Owd Roä's " master so dreaded Free Trade
that he dreamt of it, freely lamenting the " good
owd times 'at was goan " ; but he never forgot
the old dog that " coom'd thruf the fire wi' my

bairn i' 'is mouth ''; to whom we also would
give Christian burial.

The companion pictures of animal life in
rusticity have each their own place in all our
hearts.

Finally, to this interval belong the noble
verses which share with Browning's contemporary '' Epilogue '' the throne of epitaphs.
'' Crossing the Bar '' came in a moment.
Written at eighty-two, and by his own wish
now printed at the end of all editions of his
poems, it remains triumphant witness of his
courage and faith. Trusting in his Pilot, '' that
Divine and Unseen who is always guiding us,''
he would have '' no moaning at the bar,'' ''no
sadness of farewell '' when he puts out to sea.
He is ready '' to see his Pilot face to face.''

XIII

TENNYSON'S old age, like his youth and
manhood, afford but slender material
for the biographer, save in detail. His
life was at no time dramatic ; his character,
tastes and pursuits were always single-minded,
consistent, and, in a sense, limited. He never
entered into public life or literary controversy.
Though an excellent traveller, and always in-
terested in knowledge and progress, it may be
said roughly that his life was spent in talking,
reading and writing—mainly, of course, the last.
He was an admirable conversationalist when in

the mood, whether it were gossip, criticism, anec-
dote or philosophy : a sympathetic reader, with
enthusiasms and prejudices. The atmosphere
in which he lived took concrete form in the
" Metaphysical Society " founded in 1869 by
himself, Mr. Pritchard and Mr. Knowles, on the
initiative of the last-named. Its object was
friendly discussion, rather than set controversy,
between Christians and agnostics ; each party
being at that time stirred almost to fighting
point by daring deductions from evolution.
Tennyson on the one hand always welcomed
scientific advance, and on the other respected
doubt. What he deplored was the encroach-
ment, as he held then, of materialism into
spiritual affairs, and the animosities bred by
mere difference of opinion. The society wished
to ventilate new ideas without misunderstanding
the old.

Practically every member was a man of
distinction, and the list given in Lord Tennyson's
" Life " of his father is most impressive. It
includes Gladstone, Robert Lowe, John Morley
and Mr. Balfour ; Dean Stanley, James Mar-
tineau, Ward, Manning and F. D. Maurice ;
Seeley and Froude ; Henry Sidgwick and James
Sulley ; Huxley, Tyndall and W. K. Clifford ;
Ruskin, Frederick Harrison, Mark Pattison,
Leslie Stephen, and Dr. Andrew Clark, besides
the Archbishop of York, three bishops, and the
Dean of St. Paul's.

As Tennyson humorously expressed it,
" Modern science ought at any rate to have

taught men to separate light from heat," and
this struck the keynote of their meetings, at
which were discussed such subjects as the
sciences, objective and moral, physical and
social ; immortality, conscience, and the personality of God. "The Higher Pantheism"
was read at the first meeting.

For himself Tennyson respected sincerity in
every form and would have all creeds "pull together." He felt that the power of "an organized
religion" was needed by mankind, wishing the
Church of England to embrace the sects. The
society taught him that modern theologians
were more open-minded and more enlightened
than their predecessors ; without weakening his
distrust of "pure materialism," however much
he might admire its upholders. It met no more
after May 1880, "because after ten years of
strenuous effort no one had succeeded in even
defining the term metaphysics."

That such men should wish to group themselves for a common object reveals a characteristic of the age, which was marked in Tennyson, of mingling politics, science, history, and
philosophy in the one aim of helping and fixing
faith. The sudden development of science and
civilization roused a general attempt to correlate
knowledge philosophically, and bred a fancy that
men might finally solve the riddle of life.
Experts in these days were not so highly
specialized : they watched each other with
intelligence, looking for help in their own work
from every direction. It still seemed possible

for one man's mind to embrace all progress, thereby saving his own soul.

Martineau thought that Tennyson's poetry " created, or immeasurably intensified, the susceptibility of religious reverence among thousands of readers previously irresponsive to anything Divine " ; while it exerted " a dissolving influence upon the over-definite dogmatic creeds." By exposing the history of his own soul he " told the story of an age which he thus brought into self-knowledge."

The poet, however, was left a little behind at last. The modernism with which we are now familiar spelt chaos for him. His last vision of earth [1] was

> Teeming with liars, and madmen, and knaves,
> And wearied of autocrats anarchs, and slaves,
> And darken'd with doubts of a Faith that saves,
> And crimson with battles, and hollow with graves.

Yet after the vision came peace :

> For moans will have grown sphere-music,
>   Or ever your race be run !
> And all's well that ends well,
>   Whirl, and follow the Sun !

But Tennyson never admitted the mastery of continuous depression. His was a happy life, always largely dependent on family and friends. As many of these " crossed the bar " his thoughts must have dwelt much on memories of youth, since the " dialect " poems are nearly all derived

[1] In "The Dreamer," the last verses he ever wrote.

from his father's Lincolnshire parish ; but, on the other hand, he remained on almost intimate terms with Royalty, and loved to watch the stirrings of young enthusiasm everywhere. As his son happily expresses it, " true genius is seldom frozen by age."

His " crossing " was dignified and peaceful. Almost his last words witness the two passions which had most deeply inspired his work and life : " Where is my Shakespeare ? I must have my Shakespeare ! " and, again, " I want the blind up, I want to see the sky and the light."

It is surely a fact beyond dispute that, in revolting against the popular enthusiasm for Tennyson, " superior " persons have shown themselves no less conventional and narrow-minded than those whose judgment they so fondly congratulate themselves upon despising. There is, after all, a very simple explanation of what made him at once great and limited, at once beloved of many and scorned by a few.

Emotionally, Tennyson was as truly and deeply a lover of Beauty for her own sake as the most admired among the moderns. His joy in song was intense, his instinct for form was un-erring, his passion for solitude was notorious. He never felt, thought, or worked—save at his own bidding. But to him self-expression was not sufficient. He desired always to give what he most valued, to reveal his visions. It was his ambition to make others love beauty, deliberately to become the nation's poet. He was at once an artist and a preacher, a genius and a gentleman.

For though brusque and sensitive in private life, his solitariness bred in him contempt of no man. He achieved the miracle of reading poetry into the most unpoetical idealism : of expressing the most spiritual in the most material.

" Tennyson in fact was the high priest of a complacent, liberal, scientific, peace-loving, and prosperous civilization. He loved England, while abusing the demons of commerce and luxury ; he honoured God and the Queen, while extolling ' honest doubt ' ; he considered farmers the backbone of the race ; he gloried in progress as defined by the great Liberal Party." He was a mid-Victorian and a Poet.

It is because we to-day would fain deny the possibility of such a combination that so much mistaken enthusiasm has been admitted for Tennyson's early poems at the expense of his more mature and perfect work. We say that while the young poet contented himself with thoughtless singing he was indeed an artist : that when he attempted the expression of thought or feeling he became commonplace. Whereas in fact a life exclusively devoted—as his was—to the cultivation of language, enabled him almost constantly to obtain greater mastery over the mere music of words so much admired by the critical ; while a steady, untroubled devotion to humanity gave him ever clearer insight into the message of the age. Growth, so regulated and inspired, means artistic and philosophical development. The later, and longer, poems are technically more perfect, more beautiful, and more stimulating. The total body of work produced gives us a reflection, unique in clarity and completeness, of a very important period in our national history ; not otherwise, indeed, particularly distinguished by artistic, or spiritual, ideals ; but pre-eminently alert, progressive, and intellectual.

In those days, truly, there were giants in the land. It is easy, indeed, to smile at the bustling optimism of our fathers. We now know, perhaps, that there are flaws in the most perfect English gentleman : that the extension of Empire and education will not bring in the millennium : that machinery and commerce will never conquer the world : that science is powerless to solve the riddle of life. Nevertheless we benefit at every turn by the knowledge they so eagerly pursued, the material progress they so laboriously achieved, the speculations they so seriously discussed. As Carlyle and Ruskin preached, as Darwin and Spencer deduced, as Browning analyzed : we are and live.

Tennyson, obviously, did not strike deep in any direction. But he expressed the entire surface of things, the total effect of progress on the national temperament. He expressed it with a fine purity of style, a matchless perfection of language, and an absolutely single-minded sincerity that raises him among the mighty. For personally he had no part in the strenuous materialism he has idealized for all time. Sympathizing, he yet stood apart. Free throughout life from strain or worry, singularly fortunate in all his private relations, he was able to devote himself exclusively to his own development and to the service of his art. No man ever took himself and his work more calmly or more seriously.

The nation saw in him a poet who, caring for what moved them, rejoicing in their triumphs, and weeping for their distress, yet held up for their admiration a gracious image of possible perfection. He had faith and gave them of his own inheritance :

> O loyal to the royal in thyself
> And loyal to thy land.

BIBLIOGRAPHY

Bradley, A. C. : "Commentary on 'In Memoriam.'" (Macmillan.)

Littledale, H. : "Essays on 'Idylls of the King.'" (Macmillan.)

Luce, Martin : "A Handbook to the Works of Alfred, Lord Tennyson." (George Bell.)

Tairish, E. C. : "A Study of the Works of Alfred, Lord Tennyson."

MacCallum, M. W. : "Tennyson's 'Idylls of the King' and 'The Arthurian Story from the Sixteenth Century.'"

Van Dyke, H. : "The Poetry of Tennyson." (E. Mathews.)

Collins, J. Churton : "Illustrations of Tennyson."

Church, A. J. : "The Laureate's Country: a Description of Places connected with the Life of Alfred, Lord Tennyson."

Waugh, A. : "Alfred, Lord Tennyson : a Study of his Life and Work." (Heinemann.)

Brooke, Stopford A. : "Tennyson : His Art and Relation to Modern Life." (Pitman.)

Lyall, Sir A. C. : "Tennyson" (in "English Men of Letters"). (Macmillan.)